C000003652

Praise for #Shidduch

"#ShidduchCrisis is filled with funny, sad and poignant stories as its characters search for their bashert (soul mate)... Whether or not the readers are familiar with the shidduch crisis, they will find much to enjoy in this work."

Rabbi Rachel Esserman – The Reporter Group

"Every story prompted so much discussion."

Amazon reviewer

"These stories are laugh-out-loud funny and all too true to life. You capture the pain, the anguish, the hope, the desperation of dating in the Orthodox world, all with humor and poignancy. A really fun read."

Leah Gottfried – creator of Soon by You

"What an addicting read! The chapters here are just a couple of pages long so it's inevitable to fall down the rabbit hole of 'just one more page.'"

Goodreads reviewer

"I know all of these women, I grew up with them, and I was so happy to find them in this book. It made me want to give all of my friends a copy so that I could show them that finally, their existence and experiences have been acknowledged."

Amazon reviewer

[#ShidduchCrisis] is enjoyable, thought provoking, and absolutely hysterical. I couldn't put the book down once I started. Each story is as good as the next, and I honestly wish the book was another 200 pages. I highly recommend this book to anyone and everyone!

Goodreads reviewer

#ShalomBayis

-Short Stories

Penina Shtauber

This is a work of fiction. Names, characters, places, and incidents either are the product of the author's imagination or are used fictitiously. Any resemblance to actual persons, living or dead, events, or locales is entirely coincidental.

Copyright © 2020 by Penina Shtauber

All rights reserved. No part of this publication may be reproduced, stored in a retrieval system, or transmitted in any form or by any means, electronic, mechanical, photocopying, recording or otherwise, without written permission of the copyright owner except for the use of quotations in a book review. For more information, address:
peninashtauber@gmail.com
peninashtauber.com
www.facebook.com/shortshidduchstories

First printing 2020

ISBN 978-965-92757-1-7

Also by Penina Shtauber

#ShidduchCrisis

Husband and wife, if they are meritorious, the divine presence (Shechinah) dwells among them. If they are not, a fire consumes them.

Rabbi Akiva, Sotah, 17b

sha·lom ba·yis

/SHä'lōm,SHə'lōm/ /bīəs/

noun

The Jewish religious concept of domestic harmony and
good relations (or **shalom**) between husband and wife.

*// "I did the dishes for **shalom bayis**" //*

Author's Note

Let's talk about 'Life After Dating.'

Just married, when everything is fresh, new and laden with anticipation. When you discover the small nuances of living with another person, meshing your goals and lifestyles, and sharing everything with them.

Do they snore? Are they harboring a dark secret? Do they have secret talents?

Some of the stories you will encounter here are imagined, some are exaggerated and some exist.

They deal with the novelty of newlywed and early marriage. Everyone has their own way of doing things... and yes, some ways are better than others.

I hope the stories incite thoughts and conversation.

Happy readings!

Contents

Pregnant Pause

Cinnamon, maca, blueberry powder and a Chinese herb blend, mixed together in a tall glass of water. It was deep purple with stubborn lumps.

I shot back half the glass—and gagged. Purple liquid drizzled down my chin. Just two more gulps and I'd be done with it. I took a deep breath, closed my eyes, pinched my nose and tipped it back.

A glob of cinnamon caught me in the throat. I coughed, spraying purple droplets onto the gleaming countertops. The cinnamon was spicey thick. I felt nauseous.

Water! I stuck my face under the faucet and gulped mouthfuls of it. Finally, my mouth tasted bearable again. I shut the water and looked around.

Purple speckled everything—the window, its beige curtain, the counters, even the floor. The bag of maca tipped, spilling filmy white dust *everywhere*. The glass cup was dirty. My shirt wet, my wig drenched.

I couldn't help it, my eyes prickled. I sat down on a stiff kitchen chair and cried.

It's not fair, it's not fair, it's not fair. *It's not fair!*

I didn't want to drink dirt anymore. I didn't want to be scared of going outside just for the chance of running into that ugly neighbor Sherry with her baby carriage. I didn't want to go to my cousin Shimon's bar mitzvah next week where I'd see all the cousins and everyone would eye my belly expectantly. I didn't want any of it anymore. I just wanted to be normal.

I just wanted a baby.

The maca, cinnamon, dumb herb blend wasn't working. I'd been drinking it for a full week straight since I found out it could help with fertility. But how would I ever conceive if I felt sick all the time just from the taste of that thing! And not the right kind of sick.

I'd spent fifty dollars on these garbage ingredients at the health food store last week. Now I wrapped it up and tossed it.

The mess I would leave for later—first, I needed a long bath and a good cry.

That afternoon, I got a phone call.

"Hey, can you do me a favor?" It was Gitty, my sister-in-law. She lived ten minutes from me and was never short of favors to request.

I waited.

"My best friend just had a baby, I made her soup and have to get it to her before Yosef comes home. Would you mind picking Avi up from daycare?"

"Of course not!" I said, injecting positivity into my tone, "Not a problem. Should I watch him by me?"

"You could take him to the park... if you don't mind of course. I won't be too long."

"Of course, take your time!" I said with a smile and hung up.

Gitty was a bitch. This was just like her. At least once a week I'd get a call: "Come by and watch Avi as I cook. Please?" or, "You don't mind me leaving Avi by you? He's such a pain sometimes. You know how hard it is, the terrible twos." or, "I have a horrible headache... and you know, I'm *expecting*. Would you mind taking Avi for an hour?"

Yes. Of course. Why would I mind?

I laughed and smiled as my chest tightened and my womb hurt.

As I'd get my period again and cry again.

Four months. I've been married for a total of *four months* and nothing. My period was never even a day late.

"What's wrong with us?" I moaned to Lazer one night in bed, "why does Hashem hate us?"

"How could you say that?" he stroked my arm, "sometimes these things take time."

I shrugged off his hand and turned away, so disgusted, I barely wanted to look at him, let alone sleep with him. He was so earnest. So... dumb.

Yet, how could he possibly understand what I was going through? It wasn't *him* that got the looks from random aunts who said in that sly way, "I hope to wish you a mazal tov soon!" And even in the supermarket, from neighbors that I barely knew. "Hi, how are you?" we'd exchange pleasantries and then they'd do it—almost indiscernibly, but not to my trained eye—they'd glance at my stomach. I knew exactly what crossed their mind in that moment: *is that pouch too many knishes, or perhaps a baby? Nope, must be knishes.* And then they'd think, *why is she waiting so long? Are they having problems? Oh, I should add her to my* Tehilim *list. The poor Steins.*

"I've told Rabbi Katz to *daven* for us," Lazer said, "he's a real *Tzaddik.* Please don't worry."

"You *what*?" I turned on him, "now everyone will for sure know! This is so embarrassing. Why did you do that? Why didn't you ask me?"

"No one will know!" Lazer shot back, "besides, there's nothing to know. We're fine!"

"Clearly," I snapped and fell silent.

The silence was a tangible wall between us. *Clearly* we were fine.

"Should we..." Lazer started tentatively, "should we try tonight?"

"It won't help." That's what both of my fertility apps said. It was too late in the month. No use trying. I couldn't bear the thought of even touching Lazer anyway. He just didn't understand me.

Within minutes I heard his light snores.

Silent tears streamed down my face.

Now, I sat in the park, watching my nephew, Avi toddling to the slides, watching the other kids running and playing and falling and laughing, my chest tightening once again. Perhaps Rabbi Katz's *bracha* would work this time around. Perhaps next month I'd sit here a little less gloomy because inside my stomach a secret sprout would bloom.

"Look!" Avi called from the top of the slide. He tumbled down, his little curls bouncing. Two years old and always full of energy.

"Good job!" I smiled and ran over to squeeze him in a hug.

A half-hour later, I dropped him off at his home.

"It wasn't at all a problem," I told Gitty again, "you and Yosef always do so much for me."

That was a lie. Gitty and Yosef never helped us out, partly because we didn't need help. Lazer worked all day and I took care of the home, cooking, cleaning... but mostly waiting for morning sickness to dominate my schedule. It's better for fertility not to work too hard. So I waited.

Dinner with Lazer that evening was a tense affair.

"I want you to check your sperm," I announced as I brought the chicken to the table.

"Um," Lazer hesitated, "can you pass the potatoes?"

"Did you hear what I said?" I cried, "Do you *ever* listen to what I'm saying?"

"Darling—" he hesitated, knowing I hated when he called me *darling* when we argued. He started over, "we went through this already. We *both* went for fertility testing two months ago."

He reached across the table and passed himself the potatoes.

"And?" I didn't sit down. I stood over him with a hand on my hip.

"And we're both fine!"

"Oh," I laughed without humor, "and doctors *never* make mistakes. No. It's *not* worth double-checking. Not even this, the most important thing in our lives!"

Lazer got up and walked out of the room, leaving the potatoes untouched.

"You didn't even try the chicken!" I called and hastily served a few drumsticks onto his plate.

"I'm not hungry." He said from the other room. A moment later I heard a *sefer* crack open and knew I'd lost his attention for the evening.

Neither was I hungry. My stomach was the sort of empty no food can fill.

I left his plate on the table and packed the rest of the food away in containers.

"Baby," my mother called. It was noontime and I was all but waiting for her daily call, bored out of my mind. I'd cleaned the gleaming countertops and organized my clothes again. Then, when I finally heard the door of the apartment next to ours slam shut, and I knew my ugly neighbor was back from her shopping and I was sure to avoid her, I took the chance to go out and buy tomatoes for dinner. I could only start cooking in three hours though. Two and a half if I chopped really slowly.

"I'm not a baby. Don't call me that." The mere word was offensive.

"You'll always be my baby," my mother said brightly, "even at twenty-three and married."

"I'm twenty-two," I said sharply.

"Oh, are you? But March is your birthday month..."

"The *end* of March."

Nearly twenty-three. I got married late and now I'd have a baby late too. I was behind. Behind everyone. Each of my friends had a kid, some had two. I was painfully behind.

"Do you have any pleasant surprise to tell me?" my mom said as she did every phone call. It came in different phrases, the stabbing hints: "I can't wait for you to give me grandkids." "Imagine how you and Lazer would look mixed together—beautiful!" "I'm not getting any younger." And of course, the worst, *"you're* not getting any younger."

"Lazer and I are having issues." I blurted without thinking.

"What! You didn't say."

"Yes," I sat down and wrapped the fabric of my skirt around my finger, "we're thinking of divorce."

"What happened darling? You can't be serious."

Lazer and I haven't actually discussed divorce but after a good cry this morning that lasted a full forty-five minutes the thought crossed my mind and I wanted to see how it came across.

"We just don't communicate well..."

"Why don't you—" my mother was flustered, as she always was when confronted with conflict, "why don't you give it some time?" and then she gasped with faux surprise, "I know just the thing that helps couples! Now, I don't want to be one of those prying mothers but... did you think of having a baby? I know, I know, all the young couples want to wait nowadays, but how long can you wait? A year? Two? *Chas v'shalom*! How long can a couple be alone, just the two of them? I'm telling you from experience, a baby doesn't take away. It only adds."

No, the thought did not cross my mind. I told her. *I'll talk to Lazer about it. Thank you.*

"It must not work for us," I told Lazer that night in bed.

It took him a while to choose his words. He spoke in a tone of such gentle fear, I hated it.

"We have to keep trying, darling."

Of course. He's a man. That's all he thinks about. That's all he cares about. The act of trying, not the results. He could try all his life. I could only try for so long.

We tried and tried and tried. I hated him so much. He was broken. I was broken. Together, we were broken.

"It's not working for us," I cried. A full 134 days since our wedding day. Since the first time we tried.

That month my app made a mistake. It said I was due for my period. It didn't come.

"Are you still thinking of..." my mother said tentatively over the line, "how are things getting on with you and Lazer?"

"Oh, we're amazing!" I laughed, "Why are you even asking? You know we're made for each other!"

Present Tense

I waited for *Erev Shavuos*, the small box had been burning a hole in my pocket for the past two days—I wanted to give it to her already! To see the glee transform her tired face.

I exhaled heavily.

My wife worked too hard. Every morning she sent our darling baby Chanele to daycare, then taught until one. She taught *Navi* and *Torah* and *Dikduk* to third-graders. As if that wasn't enough, after the whole morning of teaching she went straight to tutor! She tutored the more difficult children privately until four, then picked up Chanele from daycare, tidied up our home and cooked a dashing dinner. It was always waiting for me on the table by the time I got home from *Kollel*.

But then, eating her delicious dish and sitting across from her, she'd smile an exhausted smile and my heart would ache.

"You have to relax," I'd insist.

"I don't want to worry you," she'd say delicately, "but bills add up—rent, electricity, water, food... I *need* to work hard."

"Oh Avigail," I'd say, looking at her from under my glasses, "don't you know, it is *Hashem* that provides *parnasa*."

But she continued to work hard and all I could do was watch, *and* try to quiet the nagging voice in the back of my head that said, *your wife doesn't have enough* emuna. *She doesn't believe* Hashem *will take care.*

No, I argued back to the voice, *she just understands the importance of* hishtadlus.

Now, I took the box out of my pocket, opened it and looked at the delicate bracelet inside. It was inlaid with precious gems and suddenly I was nervous it wasn't enough. This little string cost over a thousand dollars. It was the best we could afford, but Avigail deserved so much more.

"You have to show appreciation," my Rabbi said in his pre-*yontif shiur*, "The wife is doing the cooking and the cleaning and who knows what else!" the Rabbi paused and looked around at us, his *talmidim*. He had this way of speaking like he was directing every sentence toward *you*. We drank in his crucial words.

"Men don't understand a woman's need for beautiful things. How can we? We can wear the same pair of shoes for years! But women? No. They need a pair of shoes for Shabbos and a pair for walking and a pair for weddings and five just for show!"

A couple of men laughed, clearly relating. I didn't relate. My wonderful Avigail had two pairs of shoes just like me.

I thought back to Pesach when I insisted Avigail buy herself something new to wear, yet *seder* night came around and she wore the same blue dress she wore to all occasions. I wondered if that meant she was unhappy... or depressed, G-d forbid. I wondered if her family noticed that she didn't have anything new. I wondered if they blamed *me* for not providing for her.

"So don't try to understand your wife. Just try to make her happy," my Rabbi concluded his *vort*.

Shkoyach!

I went straight to *Gershon's Jewelers* and picked out the best our meager bank account could afford. Jewelry for *yontif* was a basic. I was truly slacking, only having bought my dear Avigail jewelry during *shana rishona*, but we were still newly married! A year and a half in, she still deserved to be treated like a queen. It was the little I could do to wipe those dark bags from under her eyes, to see her face light up like it used to.

A speckle of dust landed in the box, on the bracelet's soft white pillow. Just as I bit my lower lip and dabbed it with my shirtsleeve, the door opened— Avigail appeared with two bags of groceries hanging from Chanele's carriage. Chanele looked so dear and peaceful, eyes shut in a slumber. Avigail looked...

I smiled.

Avigail fumed.

"Avi," I said, my special nickname for her.

"I can't talk to you right now," she said, wheeling the carriage past me.

"But dear, what happened?" I followed her to the kitchen where she unhooked the bags and started unloading groceries. One bottle of wine, one gallon of milk...

"What happened?" she repeated brandishing the cottage cheese in her hand, "*what happened!?*"

23

This is another thing my Rabbi explained—women think with their hearts. They're not rational like us men. This kind of interaction happened often between us and I learned the best thing to do is to be patient and kind.

"I know you're stressed, it's almost *yontif*, but let's sit down and talk. You must be starved. Would you like me to prepare you something to eat?"

I hoped to *Hashem* she would say no. I'm useless in the kitchen!

"I'm busy," she said amicably but another minute of stocking the fridge, she burst, "why? I don't understand you! How could you? The Weinsteins are coming for lunch tomorrow. You invited them last minute! And you know what we have to feed them? *Bubkes!*"

That is what this was about? I laughed, relieved, "don't worry! You think they are coming here for the food? They are coming for the company! Asher was telling me what a wonderful time his wife had talking to you that time they came for Shabbos—"

"I filled the whole shopping cart," Avigail said, chillingly quiet. It was her strict teacher voice, I knew, and it worked all too well, "and when I went to pay, my card wouldn't go through. Not enough money in the account. Do you know how embarrassing that is? Do you know how mortifying?

Mrs. Rubins from *shul* was behind me in line. She asked if I need to borrow money—"

"She's just being a *mensch*—"

"I had enough at the beginning of the week! I checked our account! *WHERE DID THE MONEY GO*?" she bellowed.

Some things you just can't know while dating. I could have never imagined my delicate Avigail having a temper. A year and a half into marriage, and I was well aware.

That's when she noticed the box, still in my hand.

"What's that?" she demanded.

But this was not how I imagined giving the gift. I pictured it calm and relaxed, the whole house clean and Avigail ready to light candles. I imagined her tinkling laughter bouncing off the walls and—

"What is that box?" she repeated, but she already knew the answer. She was waiting for me to say it.

"I just wanted... I wanted to get you something nice for *yontif*. I know you work so hard."

For a moment Avigail smiled and I felt my heart give a triumphant leap. But then... she burst into tears.

"Return it."

"But..."

"We can't afford it now. I—thank you for thinking of me but please..." her voice trembled in an effort to remain cordial.

But her tears, the yelling, it was all too much. I snapped back.

"You should know, we won't be any happier if I give it back. What's all my learning worth if *my own wife* doesn't believe *Hashem* will help?"

It was true. It had been on my mind for months and finally, I spit it out. She worked and worked and worked. Where was her *emunah*?

Avigail looked up and met my eyes. Hers were heartbreakingly red-rimmed, mine wide and earnest through thick lenses.

I continued before she could speak, "you think that you are the only one in this house working? I also work hard, Avi. I work hard for *both* of us. I work hard for us to have a home filled with *emunah*. It's not enough to theoretically believe in *Hashem*, we have to live it too. In a way that Chanale sees it, and *im'yirzeh Hashem*, our future children too."

"What does the bracelet have to do with this?" she said, meekly.

"It has everything to do! *Hashem* wants me to show you, my darling wife, how much I care. And I care so much about you. I want you to know that."

Her lower lip trembled, eyes blinking back tears. I knew I said the right things. Avigail stepped closer and picked up her thin wrist, waiting patiently. I unclipped the golden chain from the box and wound it around her wrist. It sparkled against her freckled skin and I felt content.

She looked at it, her disgust barely disguised. But I knew I did the right thing. This was a wonderful gift for my *aishes chayil*. She just didn't know how to accept what she deserved.

"Next *yontif*," she started and sighed, "just please don't go buying things without me. If it's so important to you... I'll just choose something silver plated."

That *Shavuos*, we didn't have a lot of food on the table, Avigail and I didn't speak much—but there was really no need! The Weinsteins knew that this was a couple that loved each other and loved serving *Hashem*.

In the afternoon Avigail sat with Chanele on the couch. The baby toyed with the bracelet on her mother's wrist and I grinned.

My rabbi said you can't understand women but I find they're pretty straight forward. Even if they don't want to admit it, they love new things!

A Private Affair

"I can't find my suit," Dan said as he tossed his immaculately folded socks into his small suitcase. He looked up with a raised brow, "you picked it up from the cleaners, right?"

My hands were full of baby toys I'd collected. I let them drop back to the floor as I slapped my forehead *hard*. How could I forget? *How*? It was only written on my to-do list— twice! I dropped it off yesterday and paid extra for express. And how did I forget? Ela had a tummy ache this afternoon.

I sat with her in the doctor's office for two and a half hours and just for the doctor to tell us: "Ela's a big girl, right? She'll drink water from her sippy-cup and she'll feel better."

Thank you, Dr. Gold. Sound advice, nothing I couldn't have picked up from a quick Google search.

I rushed home, barely a minute to breathe, and put the roast in the oven. The timer dinged just as Dan came through the door, much to my relief. But Dan didn't even stop to eat.

"I have to pack," he announced. "Let's do dinner in an hour?" He looked at his watch, "make that two."

My stomach grumbled, I ate a banana and left the roast in the oven to keep it hot. Didn't Dan know I didn't like eating past seven in the evening? Ever since Ela's birth two years ago, I've been on and off diets trying to shed the stubborn weight. Only recently did I feel confident to start wearing my tighter dresses from pre-Ela days.

But the suit! How could I forget? Dan even texted me at lunchtime to make sure I'd remember. I chewed my lip and thought aloud, "okay, it's fine. I'll run to pick it up now!"

Dan slowly drew his eyes from me to the vintage clock on the wall. I followed his gaze. Already seven. The cleaners closed at four. I was acting dumb, acting dumb and I knew it.

"I'm so sorry! I can't believe it," I blurted out in a rush, "time just flew by, you know how it is. I was with Ela and then—whatever. I know it doesn't matter—"

"—It's okay, babe!" he laughed, "I'll just pack another one."

I laughed along with him, still mentally beating myself up. He did have another five suits lined up in his closet but I knew he liked his Saint Laurent suit best—the luxury fabric fell perfectly on his frame.

He stood up from the bed and paused in front of me on his way to the closet, appraising me.

His wife.

I looked back up at him, at his hazel eyes and slanted cheekbones. Ela had his eyes and his facial structure, my freckles and soft brown hair. She'd be beautiful. I hoped she'd have his confidence too. The kind of confidence that had everyone in the room hanging onto his every word. I hoped she'd have his confidence and use it for good.

"What's that smell?" he said.

"Oh," I blushed, "I may have put on some perfume. The Dior one. Remember, you chose it for me in Paris, on our honeymoon? You're right, I do think it fits me well."

"No—something's burning."

I smelled it too.

"Oh no, the roast!" I dashed down the stairs and opened the oven. A wave of heat and smoke hit me in the face. My eyes teared up as I waved the smoke away. My perfect roast, I groaned, the skin was crisped black. I placed it on the stovetop with oven mitts and stabbed it with a fork. The inside was still good. I sighed and went about the surgery to salvage dinner.

"I don't like to think of you, alone for Shabbos," I said as I always did when he had to fly.

"I'll be okay," he said as *he* always did when he had to fly, "I have lots of connections with families in Los Angeles. And you know how it is, if I don't spend Sunday on the golf course with a buyer, I'll never close a deal."

Dan was really good at what he did. What he did exactly, I wasn't sure. Something with real estate projects that involved really rich investors. Dan explained it to me once, but I asked too many questions and he got exasperated.

"You don't have to understand everything I do, okay? Just know your husband makes good money. I want to be able to provide everything for you. I want you to be happy."

I was more than happy. I was proud of him.

I hugged him at the doorstep and waited for him to lean in for a kiss. Dan was adamant about showing affection around the baby. He said it solidified her trust in love.

But Ela wasn't here. The hug was short. There was no kiss. The taxi arrived and honked from the street.

"I'll see you, babe. Tell Ela Daddy will bring her presents."

Ela was long sleeping. Dan read to her and sang to her as I watched adoringly. He already promised her presents himself, countless times.

"I will, but don't spoil her," I said.

"Can I spoil you?" he said with a wry smile.

I couldn't speak. I stole a quick peck before he turned to go.

"Stay safe!" I called after him, "tell me when you land! I miss you already! Love you!"

He waved as he got into the taxi, the driver stowed his luggage safety in the trunk, "love you."

It was all I needed to hear. I closed the door, feeling alone but a little more consoled. My husband did so much for his family.

"Mama!" Ela shrieked from the high chair. She slapped her hands down, spraying yogurt everywhere. The weekend was long. Extremely excruciatingly long. We ate at my parents which was always stressful.

"I don't like how he leaves you alone," my mom pried

"I hear he just closed a great deal in Detroit. He's going to turn that city around," my father said fondly.

And there I was, stuck between the two of them and trying to feed my baby chicken while she'd rather it land on the floor.

Sunday came and passed. Park slides and a playdate with the neighbor. Ela was only two but her social life was demanding.

And then finally it was Monday. I checked Dan's flight, it was scheduled to land in a few hours, at eight P.M. That meant his taxi should crawl up our driveway at nine-thirty latest.

I fed Ela and put her in her play-pen. She seemed happy enough—that meant I had twenty minutes before she would start whining.

Twenty minutes to relax? I wish. Maria, our cleaning lady, only came on Thursdays but I wanted the house to be spotless for when Dan arrived. I went about cleaning the house, dusting the mahogany bookshelf in the living room, and making sure the silver candlesticks, menorah and

Kiddush cups were polished to perfection. I checked on Ela, "good girl," I lulled and continued cleaning.

I swept the downstairs, the steps and the rooms upstairs. Dan's office was at the end of the hall upstairs. It's been weeks since I've tidied up there. Dan likes his privacy with work. Still, I hated to think of coffee mugs left behind there. He shouldn't be bothered with those kinds of things.

I cracked the door open and put on the lights. I loved his office. It was so—I inhaled deep wood, coffee and was that patchouli?—so manly, with a big desk and black leather chair. Dan was a real man. Twenty-five when we got married and I was just eighteen. He had a promising career ahead of him but I didn't care about that. I was just crazy about his dazzling eyes. I also had a good job back then. After Ela, I extended my maternity leave. It's been two years now. I knew I should go back to work but it's just hard sitting in a boring office when you know it's just for show. When you know your husband can easily support your whole family and that small office you worked for gets on fine without you.

I wondered what Dan thought of that. When we got married, I was ambitious too. And always ready for excitement. Dan was exciting. He showed me Paris, showed me London, took me to Broadway shows and his favorite rooftop bars. I never really went to bars before, or drank in general. Now every Shabbos we'd have a new wine on our table that he'd urge me to try, describing the difference between Merlot and Chardonnay, explaining what full-bodied meant and how to decipher what was good and bad when everything tasted the same. He never said anything about my ignorance of culture. He always loved me for me—for the little I had to offer. Not only that, but he also readily offered so much of himself.

I dragged my rag along his desk, carefully polishing around his things—scraps of paper and little notes. I didn't want to mess anything up. But still, those stubborn corners out of reach, now was my only chance. I moved his keyboard and mouse—

Something happened. The desktop hummed into life. The big screen flashed on in accordance.

I almost continued polishing, but then I stopped and dropped the rag...

Why didn't Dan have a password to stop me from logging in? And what did I expect to find when I knowingly pressed his keyboard? Not this. This was a scene from a bad movie. The empty office, the Facebook page opened on the screen where he'd left it last.

It was like one of those horrible movies. The stupid ones I tried not to see. I took a deep breath and laughed at myself. Classic dramatic me. I was always quick to conclusions.

The dark-skinned beauty smirked from her profile picture, palm trees flaunted behind her. Lior Levy.

This woman on screen must be a co-worker or a lucky co-worker's wife. Dan and she just spoke professionally. Strictly formal. Or... they didn't even speak at all. He must have heard her name and ran an innocent search.

But the chat was opened in the corner of the screen. I didn't want to look but my eyes forced me, they drank in every word.

From downstairs, Ela whined.

Lior: *When will you be here babe? I'm waiting.*

That text bubble was accompanied by a photo and I swear, I threw up in my mouth.

Lior Levy had really fine legs. *Baruch Hashem.* Good for her. Really fine, long, smooth, tanned legs.

Dan replied with a heart-eyed emoji! Yes! My inexpressive husband. Was it stuffy in here? I needed air. It couldn't breathe.

Dan: *I can't wait*

Ela's wails shocked me into focus. I ran out of the office and shut the door behind me, wishing I could just as easily shock my memory to zap out those last two minutes.

"She's Israeli, beautiful, lived in L.A. for two years." I thought back to her golden thighs in tight shorts, "not religious at all. And she's also smart! She works there as a computer engineer."

I shook Ela in my arms to soothe her. Usually, I'd looked at her face to gauge whether she'd understood anything us 'big' people were saying. Now, I hoped to God she didn't.

"This isn't the first time he's traveled. To L.A.," I added.

Raquel paused for a long time on the other end of the line, "are you sure?" she finally said again, "like *sure*, sure?"

I had all but seen them at it, "positive."

"Well," Raquel paused again, "listen, and don't take this the wrong way… it could be worse."

"*Excuse* me?"

"Not in a bad way!" she said indignantly, "but how long are you married—two years? Three?"

"You're married for five! Does your husband cheat on you?" I snapped. Ela flinched in my arms and let out a big long wail.

"Oh baby," I crooned, "I'm sorry, Mommy's so sorry."

Even Ela hated me. I dug my nails so deep into my skin I bled.

"My husband is short and fat and knows what he can get. Not like Mr. GQ you have over there." Raquel laughed in a short burst, "Men can be like that. *Especially* successful attractive men. But he's still with you, right? It means he loves you."

I thought back to the beginning of our marriage. The way he'd look at me like I was his prize, the words he'd say: "you're not like other women. I love that so much about you. You don't try to impress me, you're always so... simple. So real."

I *did* try to impress him. I'd switch from my worn errand clothes to a cute dress before he'd get home. I'd pack him lunch for the day and cook his meat how he liked it.

"It's a phase," Raquel continued even though I wished she wouldn't, "he'll get over it. Look, you're lucky, he's being decent about it choosing a woman across the country, unlike poor Dana Sharoff. You know the story, right? Her husband went off with that lady—Ziona was it? Anyway, it was all anyone could talk about. They're still together—Dana and her husband—but now *everyone* knows."

I knew the Sharoffs. I didn't know that particular story. My cheeks flamed as I thought of it—Raquel on the phone with another one of her friends—she had a lot of friends— now I would be the subject: *"what could she expect marrying a stud like that? I always wondered what he saw in her. She's a bit mousy, isn't she? Very Plain Jane."*

Why did I tell Raquel? How could I have kept it in?

"I can't—" I croaked, "I can't do it." the room was spinning. Ela felt heavy in my arms. She was playing with the pendant around my neck. It was a diamond heart and Dan gifted it to me for our first anniversary. It was so beautiful. Ela was so beautiful. This house was so beautiful. How could it hold such dirty secrets?

Ela pulled the diamond hard. The chain ripped. She giggled. I wriggled the diamond out of her fingers before she could put it in her mouth.

"Don't be silly, you *can* do it and you will. For Ela. And for you too. You're pretty helpless without him."

"I am?"

"He gives you money, he gives you kids, pays the bills for that townhouse of yours. That's a lot more than half the good-for-nothing husbands out there will give."

And suddenly I felt like the dumb little girl I was.

"Just act like you don't know. Men hate drama. Let him do his thing. I'm telling you, it's a phase. Like Dana and her man. You guys will get over it."

I nodded and nodded, thanked her for her advice and time. Always a good friend. Always knew what to say. My cheeks stinging from the metaphorical slap in the face each time I visualized sexy Lior Levy and that stupid heart-eyed emoji response.

"Remember," she said before she clicked off, "whatever you do, *don't* confront him."

I was left with the silence of the too-big house. It was six-thirty. That left me three hours. I collected the broken necklace chain and diamond and put it in a cup beside my candlesticks. We'd have to get that repaired. I fed Ela. I put her for her nap even though it was too late to nap, laid on our huge bed, on Dan's side, inhaled his scent, curled up in a ball and imagined him curled around me, even though he didn't like doing that, and cried. I cried because he didn't like cuddling. I cried because he spoke to me like I was a little girl and didn't understand. I cried because I was a little girl and didn't understand—didn't understand why anyone would want to hurt their wife so badly. Why anyone would be so dissatisfied, they couldn't talk about it, they'd rather jet to L.A.

We could have gone to counseling. I could have changed. I could have dieted better and worn high heels more often. I thought he wanted me simple, I thought he liked me that way.

Lior. Lior, Lior, Lior. She was worldly, otherworldly even. Exotic and smart. The type of woman that slept with other women's husbands and didn't mind it one bit. Probably preferred it that way. Probably enjoyed bending the rules of monogamy.

My phone dinged to tell me a half-hour passed. I wiped my tears, blew my nose and did my makeup. Then I went down to prepare a grand dinner. I always made Dan his favorite foods when he came home from a long trip—my breath hitched—I just knew he worked so hard.

By the time the table was set, Ela bathed and dressed in jammies, the house spotless and shining, a car rolled down our block.

Finally, Dan was back. His tall presence dominated the living room, breathing soul into the walls. It was good to have a man in the house. He scooped up Ela in his arms. She beamed. He hugged me close and I tried to imagine these arms around someone else. If Dan noticed me stiffen, he didn't say anything.

The conversation over dinner was smooth and casual.

"Mr. Loafer was very pleased with my offer," Dan drawled, "I have to fly back again soon to finalize things." I choked and drank water to cover it up. He continued, "but it seems like we'll be ready and set to start in May. Of course, I'll have to stick around a bit to overlook the construction."

"I'm so happy it worked out for you. And for Shabbos, was it okay?"

"As I said, the community is very welcoming."

Did I imagine the glint in his eye?

Dinner was a painful affair. I dug my nails into my forearms to make it bearable.

Later that night Dan crawled into bed beside me. He leaned to whisper into my ear, "please don't go into my office again."

He touched my back and I wondered if he would continue. But then he rolled over and fell asleep.

Biting my lip so I wouldn't cry out loud, I repeated the words he once told me like a mantra in my head: *"You don't have to understand everything I do."*

Social Security

"Happy birthday!" Chedva said over the phone. Her call surprised me—my older sister never called.

"Wow, you remembered."

We had lived in the same house celebrating it together for fourteen years. But it's been eleven years since. Chedva got married, had six kids by now and a lot on her mind. I wouldn't blame her if she'd forgotten. I barely remembered when her birthday was. Sometime in *Nisaan*...

Chedva laughed, "of course I didn't! I saw Aliza's post. Wow, she's so sweet. You know, you're a really lucky man."

"Yes, I know," I said, smiling at the mention of my wife, "but what post?"

"On Instagram. You didn't see it yet?"

"I'll have to check it out."

We spoke a few more minutes—how are the kids doing? Is Shimon all right in school? fifth grade—wow, when did he get so big? And Chaviva is already in gan!

How is my Aliza doing? She feels great! Four months pregnant already. Yes, the first trimester was harder... Okay, Chedva, why don't you call her and tell her all this pregnancy stuff yourself?

I spoke on autopilot because my mind was busy focusing on two things: 1) I didn't *have* Instagram. 2) I *had* to see this post.

It was easy enough to find her. I downloaded the app and typed her name in the search bar. It was the first option @alizajasper101.

I clicked on her account. It loaded pictures and all.

The post I was searching for out of 1,276 posts wasn't hard to find. It was the newest one: A picture of me from our honeymoon. I had a fresh haircut, a new shirt and was laughing at something out of the frame. But the colors were bolder here. The ocean brighter, my skin tanner—as if the photo was put through a warm lens. Underneath was a long caption.

To the bestest husband in the world! We've been together through thick and thin. Through the good and the best of times. Sometimes I stop and wonder, what was life without you? How is it possible that just a year ago, by your last birthday, we were practically strangers? And now, you're my best friend and favorite person in the whole wide world. I can't imagine a life without you in it. No matter how dark the skies may seem, I think of my hubby, know you're there for me and everything is all right. Thank you so much for being YOU, you make me be a better ME. Here's to you on your very special birthday! And to many more on this wonderful journey we're on together called life! Love you to the moon and back. XOXO-@alizajasper101

My heart swelled with conflicting emotions. It was the single sweetest letter anyone had ever written to me... yet she didn't write it to me. She wrote it to the internet.

I scrolled through her photos. I was in a lot of them—at the wedding, we went to last week, one from our hike on Friday, two from our outing to that quirky café, one dressed for Shabbos in the setting Friday sun. There were many of her alone too, some of which I recognized because I myself had photographed them. There were some in the mirror, or a selfie, her lips bright with lipstick and the caption always inspiring:

Shoot for the stars, or, *you don't know what you're capable of*, or, *don't let the bad days get you down.*

And there was food, so much food! That shakshuka breakfast which she surprised me with last month, a smoothie she got with friends, restaurants, outings, dinner, events—

I closed the app, shut my phone and felt... cheated?

That evening, as we prepared avocado toasts for dinner—neither of us had the energy to cook—I waited for Aliza to bring it up. We sat at the table and she still didn't say anything. Although she did stop to photograph her plate, something she always did but I barely noticed. Until now that is. Until I saw them neatly edited and captioned in that vague inspiring way.

"Chedva called today," I mentioned.

"Oh, what about?" Aliza glanced at something on her phone.

"She wanted to wish me a happy birthday."

"Oh right! Yeah, happy birthday," she smiled at me, "wow, you're so old," then she looked back at her phone.

"I'm not old," I said indignantly, "I'm twenty-five."

"That's a quarter of a century... sounds pretty old to me."

We ate our toasts in silence. I waited for her to speak again. To say something about my birthday... but she probably planned a surprise—it was the first of either of our birthdays together married. Maybe she'd say or do whatever it was later, tonight. Maybe she'd surprise me next week, on my English birthday. Maybe she'd give me a card and a present, maybe she'd take me out on Thursday night. Maybe she planned a dinner with my friends.

Patiently impatient, I waited all night.

Patiently impatient, I waited all week too.

Aliza did not bring up my birthday again.

"I don't get it! Why didn't you say anything?"

Two weeks passed, both birthdays, Hebrew and English, gone. No dinner, no present, no event, no words. We sat at the table, dinnertime, waiting for my lasagna in the oven.

I couldn't keep my feelings in any longer.

"I told you happy birthday!" she said indignantly, "didn't I?"

"I saw your post," I said eventually.

"Oh, good! I knew I did *something* for your birthday,"

"I don't have Instagram! How did you expect me to see it?"

"Clearly you managed all right."

"I just don't get why you couldn't tell me these things to my face. Why can you tell everyone in the world but me? *About* me?"

She opened up her phone and scrolled on her Instagram, stopping on my birthday post, "*awww*, I am so sweet! Of course, I want everyone to know how I feel about you! Why is that a problem?"

"It's not a problem..." I said, but it was a problem. I just couldn't explain why. In the end, I said, "I like when things are more private."

"*You* are an introvert," she pointed, "and *I* am an extrovert."

"That has nothing to do with it! Just don't post stuff like that. Please. I'd much rather you write it on a card and give it to me."

"It's not one or the other," she folded her arms, "of course you can't accept me as I am. I do something nice and it backfires in my face."

"I do appreciate it!" I snapped remembering those sweet words she wrote about me, "I just don't get why you can't tell me to my face."

The timer dinged on the oven. Aliza disappeared to the kitchen. She came back in five minutes with placemats and silverware. I helped her set the table as she brought out a jug of orange juice and then our lasagna in its steaming dish. She served a piece for each of us on ceramic dishes.

I took a deep breath and tried to forget about all this, just relax and have a nice dinner together—but then Aliza stepped onto her chair with her phone at hand, lifting it to capture it all in the frame.

"No!" I said, slamming my fist on the table, "Let's just enjoy our food without taking a picture of it."

Aliza stopped and looked down at me, "you're being really ridiculous, you know?"

"Me?" I laughed, "I'm being ridiculous? I just want to eat!"

"How long does it take to take a picture? Ten seconds? We've waited for a half-hour, another ten seconds is going to kill you?"

"Yes!" I jumped to my feet to be level with her, "Yes, because you're going to post it. Post it and show the world our damn dinner. Just like you posted about my birthday, about Rafi and Shira's wedding last week, about breakfast, lunch and supper and every other moment of your day!"

"Why do you care so much? I like it. I enjoy it. Stop getting involved."

"So stop involving me," I said, "This is the last time I'm going to eat with you if you keep taking pictures. *Okay?*"

"Okay," she mumbled, "one picture though, it looks so good."

She snapped a photo and came down from the chair.

"Stop being mad at me," Aliza said the following evening. I tried to hide how I felt, but last night I sneaked onto her Instagram and saw our dinner with another glowing caption:

My husband is the best chef in the world! #lasagna

Since then I couldn't look at Aliza properly.

"It's like you're not listening to a word I say."

"Of course I am," Aliza dumped scrambled eggs from the pan onto two paper plates. She put a plate of whole raw vegetables between us with a knife stuck inside a tomato, "I told you, I'm not taking pictures of our food anymore."

The egg soaked into the paper plate, making it soggy.

"Great," I smiled, "we could still use dishes though."

"What's the point anymore?" Aliza sighed, "are you still upset? I can delete the birthday post..."

"No don't. Do whatever. I don't care."

"Okay good," she grinned, "because that post got *tons* of likes. I have to post more pictures with you—people love it!"

Just a Phase

"Oh, that's totally normal," Travis said.

"What's it been, two months?" Jed asked.

"Yeah."

Travis nodded sagely, "My wife got into 'energies' after she gave birth to Kimberly. She started spraying oils around the house, going barefoot and meditating. Don't worry," he laughed at our concerned faces, "she went back to wearing shoes after a few months."

"It could be worse," Max piqued, "my wife got depressed. She wouldn't get out of bed for weeks."

We all looked down at our beers in sympathy and took a few gulps in the name of unpredictable postpartum wives.

This is what I loved about the weekend—Friday night at the bar with the guys. This is what Jenny was trying to take away from me.

"What did you say she does exactly?" Max asked.

I sighed and tried to explain, "She started doing all this Jewish stuff. Going to classes at the synagogue and making friends with all the ladies there. She stopped buying meat for the house, says it ruins the soul."

That was just the tip of it, but my friends were already patting me on the back.

"She'll tire herself out," Travis said.

"Let her do her thing," Max added. "At least it doesn't affect you."

Jed, the unmarried guy in the group, looked thoroughly relieved. His girlfriend Sasha of five years swore she'd never have kids.

The meat thing was fine. I just ate out for my cheeseburger fix, and I was getting pretty fit off of all the salads Jenny prepared. So what was the problem?

The baby's name? His circumcision? Friday night?

Mainly, it boiled down to Jenny's obsession with this random woman, Raizel Berman.

Up until a few months ago, our life was *normal*. More than normal—it was perfect. We lived in a nice house, had good jobs and good neighbors. We were ready for a kid.

Jenny and I met seven years ago on a Birthright trip. We went to the same uni but didn't even know it until we were grouped together on the trip. I'd signed up for the girls—and they didn't disappoint. There was Ashley and Sarah and Rebecca, but the moment I saw Jenny in her black bikini, knee-deep in the Sea of Galilee, I knew I wanted her. We spent the day together, and the night, and since we were inseparable. A year later she moved in with me and five later we tied the knot, on the coast of Los Cabos. Then, we put the down payment on our two-story home and finally decided we were ready. We had the job, the house and each other. We were ready to be parents.

But then Jenny, mid-pregnancy, started bringing up this Raizel woman. At first, I didn't think anything of it.

"I met the most amazing woman at my check-up today!" And then: "That woman I was telling you about, Raizel, she invited me over for lunch." And then, "I'll be by Raizel's. She wants to teach me about different mothers in the bible." And then, "Raziel said I should meet the other women at the synagogue."

"What is this?" I asked, "Hebrew school?"

Jenny rubbed her swollen belly and smiled, "I have to know a thing or two to teach Josh. What will we do when he asks about his heritage?"

I shrugged. Heritage to me was like horoscopes. It meant a lot if you cared.

Jenny was just nervous to become a mother. She wanted to get everything right. She ordered eight different parenting books on Amazon, and read articles late past midnight differentiating high-chair styles. I went along with her to the parenting seminar, peeked at the parenting books, did some Google searches myself, but it was all too overwhelming. I figured I'd just do what all parents did with their first child—I'd wing it.

All too soon the day arrived. Hours of labor that had me cringing and loving my wife even more—Josh came into the world screaming, covered in amniotic fluid. We became parents.

Hours later, on the hospital bed, I wrapped my arm around Jenny, my beautiful hero, carefully cradling our brand new little boy. Josh. He looked so fragile merely hours old, I was almost too scared to touch him. Slowly, I reached out and stroked his tiny hand, let him grab my finger and hold on tight.

It was then that Jenny blurted out, "I don't think we should name him Josh."

"Why not?" I demanded, "We chose the name *years* ago. You don't remember? We already told everyone. Look at this boy, he is such a Josh. What else could he be?"

When we started dating, we saw a movie in theaters. We both forgot the name of it, a random action film, but the main character was named Josh.

"What a handsome name," Jenny had said.

"Our first son's name," I joked. But the joke became more real as we got more serious, eventually married, and eventually became pregnant. Once we discovered it was a boy it was decided.

Josh.

"I was thinking something more... Jewish." Jenny said eventually, "What do you think of David? Like King David"

"David?" I scoffed, "it's too... serious. He'll feel pressure all his life. Let's just stick with Josh."

Josh opened his eyes as if he knew we were deciding his fate. He'd been Josh for the past five months, I called his name regularly through Jenny's belly. He wanted to be named Josh, I could see it in his eyes. I wouldn't let some Jewish craze decide this poor baby's fate.

Jenny pursed her lips and didn't say anything. I said loudly, "Don't worry Joshy, your dad will take care of this." She didn't call him out loud, but I did hear her whispering, "Oh, little baby David," when she thought I wasn't listening.

The next day Jenny was glowing.

"Raizel said it's okay!"

"What?" that name, *Raizel*. I tensed at the mention of that woman.

"Josh," she said the name fondly, "it's a Jewish name. Joshua. He led the Jews into Israel after Moses passed on. I do think we should call him Joshua though."

"Whatever you want," I said, relieved about the name yet perturbed by this new influence on my wife's life—Raizel.

And then Raizel's name came up again. Later that day when I asked the doctor about circumcision.

Jenny pulled my sleeve.

"Your wife canceled it," Dr. Stevens said, looking back and forth between us.

When he left, I turned on Jenny, "canceled?"

"Raizel suggested we do it in the synagogue! A whole ceremony with a rabbi. It will be really fun."

"Fun? No rabbi is cutting our boy's penis!" I snapped, "Josh needs a trained professional."

"The rabbi is trained! It's going to be next Monday."

"Jenny! If we're going to do it, we have to do it now. It's nearly forty-eight hours since he was born! What are you thinking?"

"Just trust me okay, it's a Jewish thing. We'll wait eight days."

Just because she carried the baby for nine months, and now nursed life into him, she felt like she had more of a say in his life. The way she sheltered him in her arms, I was too scared to argue otherwise.

"I'm going to ask the doctor if it's okay…" I muttered and left the room.

I finally met Raizel at Josh's circumcision ceremony in a small but ornate synagogue. She was this little woman piled under layers of dark clothing. She had short brown hair and didn't shake my hand.

"The famous Raizel," I said, "I hear so much about you. Can you tell me—what has gotten into my wife?"

"I wouldn't want to gossip about your wife," Raizel said, "but I can tell you this—when a heart is lacking, it finds water at the source."

"I don't speak riddles—"

But then her husband arrived, a rabbi by the looks of his beard, and launched into conversation with me.

Where am I from, he wanted to know.

"Philadelphia."

"Before that," he said.

"The lower east side."

"Before."

"My grandparents? Great-grandparents?" I laughed, why did he care to know? "They're from Lithuania, Czechoslovakia, left during the war."

"Your mother's parents too?"

"Yeah."

The rabbi seemed pleased. I wanted to say something more but more men in white shirts, black pants, long tassels and black skullcaps filed in. It was like a cult uniform. We had to get out of here. I looked around for Jenny—easy enough to spot in her normal jeans and tank top. She was deep in conversation with drab Raizel. I groaned.

"I don't like that Raizel woman," I ranted on as Jenny rocked a crying Josh. "You see! That rabbi didn't know what he was doing. I'm telling you he cut too much."

They'd brought in a second rabbi to make the cut. An old man with a white beard, and glasses so thick I was sure he was blind.

It was too late to protest. The bearded men mumbled things and *swish* went the knife. Poor Josh. I elbowed my way through them to collect my child. Jenny beat me to it, hugging Josh close to her chest.

"He'll be okay," Jenny said with no conviction, she bit her lip and undid his diaper to look inside, "it's fine. He's fine!"

"It'll be okay," I squeezed Jenny's arm, "just never go back there. What a horrible place."

"Don't say that!" Jenny jerked back.

"What? You agreed they messed up."

"They didn't mess up. He'll be okay," she said again as if trying to convince herself.

"Out here? What do you have in mind for tonight?" I grinned. It was a Friday evening, a few weeks after Josh was born. I still heard the name Raizel every now and then but mostly things were normal. The circumcision thing threw Jenny off. It threw me off too.

Jenny set our candles up on the living room table. The ones we used for romantic candlelit sex. They were from Bed Bath and Beyond. One was sandalwood scented and the other jasmine.

She struck a match and carefully lit each candle. Then she smiled at me, "I wanted to try this for a while but I was scared I'd mess up. It's for Shabbat."

"Isn't that Saturday?" I knew *some* Jewish stuff.

"It starts tonight," Jenny said sagely, "we're supposed to have a meal."

"That's nice," I looked at my watch, "we should eat soon-ish, then I'm heading out."

"Do you have to?"

"What?"

"Head out."

"It's Friday night," I laughed wearily, "I always go out with the guys."

"Its family time, you can't stay in one week?"

They're the ones keeping me sane, I wanted to say, *you're the one driving me insane.* Instead, I firmly shook my head, "let's eat now, I'm starved."

We ate next to the flickering candles.

I cleared the table and looked back at the candles, wax melting to liquid, "do we leave them on?"

"I don't know," Jenny said, "it is kind of a waste,"

I put out the flames, "but we will light them later... right?"

What had Travis said? It's just a phase.

I repeated it like a mantra in my head when Jenny showed me her new t-shirts, three sizes too big.

"I'm trying to be a bit more modest, my regular tops are very revealing."

"What's the problem with that?" and then I remembered Raizel buried in her layers of clothes, "oh no, no, no, no. You are not going there! Buy something your own size and don't either start with baggy jeans."

I liked my wife in her skinnies. I liked her just the way she was.

It's just a phase.

Football season was back and we hosted a watching party at ours. I ordered burgers for everyone and just as I paid the delivery guy Jenny dragged me to the kitchen, Wendy's still in my hand.

"What is that? We don't eat burgers in the house!"

"So don't eat yours, who's forcing you?" I tried to push past her.

"No," she caught my arm, "throw it out. I'll make us a salad."

"Just because you're vegetarian doesn't mean the world has to be," I hissed.

"Not vegetarian," Jenny said, "*kosher.*"

Like it mattered! I gave out the burgers and Jenny wouldn't look at me all night.

It's just a phase.

Another month passed and Jenny had me stay home on Friday night.

"It's family time," she said firmly.

Max sent a picture of a tall glass of beer. *Waiting for you.*

It's just a phase.

She practiced her Hebrew an hour every night.

It's just a phase.

She really wanted me to meet with the rabbi. "Only if you want, but it would make me so happy. Just to learn a little bit. Not for you, for Joshua!"

"If Joshua wants, he could go to Hebrew school."

"Maybe we can send him to a private Jewish school?"

It's just a phase.

Promised Land

"I filled out the papers from Nefesh B'Nefesh, there are just a few things I'm missing, like your birth certificate, also your parent's *ketubah*... Ooh," Yehuda remembered, "we have to get proof of no criminal record."

"Oh no," I sighed, gutting a pepper, "you got me. Criminal record. I took your muffin last week, remember? Now they won't let us in."

"Why do you sound happy about that?" Yehuda took the pepper from me and sliced it on the cutting board, "and don't worry. I'll forgive you this time."

I rolled my eyes and ignored Yehuda's Aliya antics, "how was work? Did you speak to your boss about his after-hour demands?"

Yehuda worked nine hours a day. As if that wasn't enough, his boss expected him to answer urgent messages from clients. At first, it was fine, but suddenly every text and email was deemed 'urgent'. Even at home, Yehuda's hand was at his phone, ready to work at every given minute and it was draining for both of us.

"Actually," Yehuda chose a cucumber and peeled it carefully, "I gave my boss an early notice,"

"You did *WHAT!?*" I put down my own peeler and fumed.

"I figured, why spend another winter here? We don't have to wait for the summer to move..." he bit his nails like he always did when he was exasperated, stressed, or nervous. "We discussed this a thousand times!"

"No, I don't recall us ever discussing anything! Call your boss back and tell him you *love* your job!"

I put my share of salad in a bowl and took it to the couch, so rattled, I could barely eat.

The next day, we each came home from work, prepared dinner together as always. The air was tight with tension and I didn't have the courage to ask, "Did you tell your boss you're staying?" So instead, I decided to forgive him. I asked him questions about his day, he answered back and asked his own. We laughed, we ate. We did all the motions that reminded us of why we loved each other.

Then we were in bed, getting cozy when Yehuda brought it up again.

"Sweetie, you know it's what I wanted. What *we* wanted. We've been married over a year already..." he put a hand on my shoulder.

"So?" I shrugged his hand off, "and this is *not* what I wanted."

"Then why did you tell me it was? When we were dating. I always said I wanted to make Aliya immediately and you agreed! We've waited over a year, it's long enough."

"What are you even saying?" I ran my hands through my hair, buried my face in my palms, "I never said *I* wanted to move."

"I specifically only went out with girls who wanted to move. We literally spoke about it on our dates. Don't make me out like a bad guy."

"Oh, so coercing your wife to move to another continent where she has no friends or family is the good thing to do?" I shook my head, "and don't twist my words. I said I would *like* to live in Israel—yeah, one day I would. Who wouldn't? And don't hold something I mentioned on an hour-long date in some café over me for the rest of my life."

"It's the reason we went out."

"Yehuda!" I snapped, "Living in Israel is not practical. At *all*. Stop pretending all the time and man up."

Seminary was nice. More than just a fun year, it was a break from the city and a window into a different life. A more spiritual life. I would *like* to be on that level—wrapping ugly scarves on my head and not caring. But I wasn't. I needed New York.

"What is ever practical?"

"How about living in the country with our family, jobs, friends..." I listed off my fingers. The only family either of us had in Israel was Hoshea, Yehuda's brother.

"So why did you say you would? I just don't get you." Yehuda whispered to his lap.

"Hey," I sat up, "Didn't you say you'd quit smoking—when we were dating?"

I smiled, triumphantly. I won. I knew it. I saw it in Yehuda's eyes. He tried quitting, it lasted two weeks. He tried again, then went out for a smoke. I nagged him every now and then but nothing worked.

Yehuda pushed his blanket off and got up, crossed the room and got his Marlboros from his jacket pocket. He brought them to the bathroom—I leaned to watch—took out scissors and cut the box through. Then he ran the water over the half-cigarettes.

"No need to be dramatic about it," I called, then muttered to myself, "Let's see how long this lasts."

"Yehuda asked me for your birth certificate." My mother said over the phone. We hadn't spoken for a few days so I called her over my lunch break.

"Did you give it?" I ripped a string cheese open with my teeth.

"Well, I didn't see why not."

"Why not?" I repeated, "Do you know what he wanted it for? *Did you even ask?* To make Aliya! Do you *want* your daughter moving across the world from you?"

"...Didn't you want to live in *Eretz Yisroel*?"

I groaned and said goodbye. She was supposed to be on *my* side, supposed to *want* me to stay. Instead, she was just as positive as Yehuda that my dream life lay in Israel.

And then things took an extreme turn. Yehuda had booked us tickets, "just for a pilot trip. To see how it is." His face split into a huge grin as he told me.

"What the heck? You can't spend two thousand dollars on pilot trip tickets without consulting your wife first!" I wanted to pull out my hair, but it was safely tucked under my wig. Instead, I folded my arms, "besides, I am *not* moving."

"They were fifteen hundred dollars," Yehuda said and rushed to add, "So forget moving. Let's just think of it as a vacation. We never got to go on a honeymoon."

"Because of work—the same work we still *have*."

"I asked for the week off. I'll give you the dates so you can take off too."

"I can't just take off." I worked as a dental assistant and my boss, Dr. Feinberg was not sympathetic at all.

"Should I go alone?" Yehuda asked casually, "I'll let you know afterward if it's worth making the move."

"No thank you."

I took a week off from work. Dr. Feinberg was all too understanding. Family emergency in the holy land, he couldn't say no.

Three weeks later we landed at Ben Gurion airport. The whole plane clapped but me.

Yehuda's brother, Hoshea picked us up with his beaten car. Before we got in, Hoshea offered Yehuda a cigarette which Yehuda kindly deferred, "I actually quit. For good this time."

Hoshea lived in Israel for seven years. He'd met his Israeli wife, Moriah, while learning in yeshiva, fell in love, got married, no doubt thinking he'd convince her to move to the States. But she wanted to stay and that was that.

Hoshea was a proper husband, I thought glumly, *he wants the best for his wife*. By now they had four kids and lived in Ramot, a neighborhood in Yerushalayim.

Yehuda rode shotgun. He and Hoshea spoke animatedly the whole ride to Yerushalayim.

"...So the coffee prices tanked. Now you can get a cup anywhere for only five shekel."

"That's awesome! And coffee here is way better than that fake stuff they overprice in New York."

"Of course. *Everything* is better here."

I looked out the window and tuned them both out.

We stayed by Hoshea in a private unit attached to his building. It was the *hachnasat orchim* suite, at least that's what Moriah called it in her accented English, "you can stay as long as you like."

"Don't worry," I assured her, "we won't be here long."

Hoshea and Moriah were really sweet, so I felt bad saying this—but their apartment was hideous and cramped. Even our private unit had an old crib stored in it and boxes of baby clothes. The walls were stark white with black stains and the floor was speckled tiles. The beds were thin, it hurt just to sit on them, and the milk in our little fridge tasted weird.

My nieces and nephews—weird to think that of these kids I'd never met before—were cute in the face but dressed horribly. One had a hole in her shoe, the other had a yarmulke so faded, it looked fifth hand. Another carried his teddy bear everywhere—it looked as if it harbored dangerous bacteria in its greyed fur.

On our first evening, we had dinner together around the squashed family table. Everyone was happy and smiling and communicating in broken Hebrew and English.

The hardest part about living in a small apartment? There wasn't anywhere to cry.

The next day Yehuda left me alone. *Some honeymoon*, I thought glumly. He went with Hoshea to work and told me I should get to know Moriah a bit better. She was my sister-in-law after all and needed help around the house.

I had no interest in spending time with a woman I'd never met before and would only meet every couple of years at random family events. Instead, I took a bus to Ben Yehuda. I wanted to recall that pull I'd had in seminary. Just three years ago, what had I loved about this country?

Everything depressed me—the beating sun, a million watts strong—in September! The whitewashed stone on every building, like desert sand. The bus that people fought to get on, stuffed with so many poor moms with baby carriages. Either they had to stop having babies or they had to buy a car. The girls in the street with sandals and long *shlumpy* skirts. It was downright depressing.

I wanted fashion. I wanted single file lines and fancy cars parked on the street. I wanted seasons, especially the rich colors of New York in autumn. By now the leaves would be wilting off the trees in Central Park, deep oranges and flaming reds.

Israel knew only of the beige of its buildings, the blue of the sky and the green of the grass—unless it was summer. Then the grass turned beige too.

I wanted Starbucks. Not this slushy iced coffee that I'd bought for five shekels.

I wanted English, not broken, not aggressive. Just plain and polite English.

I tossed my iced coffee in the trash and went back to the bus stop. I really just wanted to go home.

The rest of the week passed surprisingly fast. Instead of counting the minutes, they flew by. We took Hoshea and Moriah out to a restaurant after visiting the *kotel*. The next day, we borrowed Hoshea's car and took a day trip to the north. The sea was stunning under the setting sun. We found a *tzimmer* near the Kinneret and stayed for the night. We explored Tzfat, passed through Meron, visited some *kevarim*, and drove back to Yerushalayim. We explored Yerushalayim too. The sandy city. It was fun to explore when I didn't have to picture myself or my future in this place.

Shabbos was sweet. Moriah wasn't a good cook so I insisted on helping her with the salad. That way Yehuda and I could at least have it the way we liked.

And then it was Sunday. Our flight was scheduled for that evening. Our room was a mess, the contents of our small handbags exploding on every surface.

"We could still go out today, but let's pack up first," I said.

Yehuda didn't answer, sprawled flat on the bed and staring at the ceiling.

"No way am I packing for you," I prodded him as I folded my own clothes.

"I'm not going back," Yehuda said the sentence so nonchalantly, I almost didn't hear.

"Excuse me?" I stopped folding my blouses and looked up sharply.

"I like it here. I like Yerushalayim. I spoke to Hoshea, we can stay here as long as we need, until we can settle. I also spoke to his boss. He agreed to take me on for a short term project, see how I do, but he's willing to hire me full time. You can help Moriah out with her daycare until you find something better."

"We came to test it out. I don't like it. I don't want to live here," I said firmly, "and I will *never* ever work in a daycare. Don't say anything that dumb ever again."

"So go back," he shrugged, "I'm staying. I keep my word."

"We are married! Some word you keep—pleasing your wife." I scoffed.

"Of course I'll please you, in Israel, like we planned. Or should we be miserable in New York?"

"Are you threatening me?"

76

"Are you threatening *me*?"

I crossed the room and came real close to my husband, "if you don't come home with me, I'll cry. I'll cry until my eyes are red and you will be miserable. We both will be."

"It's your choice to be miserable or not," he said in that infuriatingly calm way.

I wanted to slap him. An overwhelming urge.

"It's your choice."

I packed my bag. I packed his bag. We were ready to leave.

I didn't get on the plane. As much as I threatened, I couldn't fly without him.

"We'll go back," he assured me, "we still have to bring our things. But not now. Now let's enjoy. I'm sure we can get our *Teudat Zehuts* as soon as this month!" he sighed, "I know it's hard now, but you love Israel! Remember what you said about seminary? It was the best year of your life. You said you were the most connected to Hashem you ever were. You're going to love it here, I just know."

He said those words in Hoshea's dinky *hachnasat orchim* suite. The window was frosted because it faced the street. And I suddenly felt so trapped.

Yehuda glowed.

I cried.

Urgent Care

"Can you come home early tonight?" Michal asked over the phone.

Leave work early? I let out an incredulous laugh—I barely had time to answer the phone! Still, I glanced at my schedule to confirm what I already knew: from lunch till six was packed with meetings and that was besides a project I had to complete.

"It's really not the best day," I admitted, "the rest of the week is a little less crazy though, I can try tomorrow..." That was an overstatement. The rest of the week was just as crazy but tomorrow's five o'clock meeting was adjustable, and I could work through lunch if I had to.

Michal sighed heavily, "Levy isn't feeling well and I can't get him to calm down."

I bit my finger. An email popped up as URGENT on my screen and I had to meet with my supervisor in three minutes to show him sketches I barely had time to complete.

"I can't do this myself," Michal groaned, "this is ridiculous." As if on cue, Levy's wails filled the line.

Now it was two minutes to the meeting with my supervisor. My wife needed me at home early. I looked at my schedule, packed with barely a moment to breathe and scribbled myself a reminder at the last hour. How on earth could I miss that meeting with the interior team?

"Okay, okay," I promised, "I'll be there."

In the end, I went to the last meeting for the first ten minutes, looked at my phone, mumbled something about, "family emergency," and bolted. It wasn't okay. I couldn't do it again. But today Michal needed me so I'd make the exception.

On the drive home, I thought about Michal, what it must be like to be home with Levy all day—his crying, complaining, poopy diapers—and felt guilty. I worked at an architecture firm, long hours, intense and exhausting, but I loved it. I loved watching how a project came together like pieces of a puzzle, I loved being part of that puzzle and mainly, I loved how I was able to support my family doing it. But what good is that if your family resents that you're never around?

I clenched the steering wheel and resolved to work through lunch this week to make it home earlier.

"Michal?" I hung the keys on the hook and stepped inside the dark house. No answer. I walked through the living room, flipping the lights on as I did.

"Hey," she said. I jumped.

Michal was splayed out on the leather loveseat in an oversized t-shirt, one headphone in, holding her cell phone above her face. She peeled an eye away to greet me.

"Where is Levy?" I asked, "Is everything all right?" his toys were scattered on the rug, colorful blocks disappearing under the couch.

"Oh yeah," she yawned, "he fell asleep hours ago. Oh, maybe wake him up so he doesn't keep you up all night?"

I'd wake up at night for Levy. It was only fair as Michal tended to all his needs during the day. Except, sometimes that meant staying up half the night and depending heavily on coffee and the mercy of Hashem to keep my eyes open during the long meetings and hours in front of the computer screen. I chewed my finger, already nervous for tomorrow.

"You said he wasn't feeling well?" I pressed.

"Yeah!" finally she put her phone aside and sat up, "he was crying for twenty minutes straight. I had no clue what to do with him! But then he burped and chilled out. Thank G-d."

"Oh, thank G-d," I laughed, hoping it didn't edge hysteria as I glanced at my watch. They'd be wrapping up the meeting about now. Did Michal notice I came home early? She looked back at her phone, tapping the screen intently.

I jogged upstairs and lifted a fretful Levy from his crib. He was one and a half and big for his age. I gently prodded him until he blinked his eyes open and threw his head back in a whine.

"No," I insisted, righting him up, "you're staying awake now. It's not bedtime yet."

This kid had the worst of schedules, Michal always complained to me, he woke up late and napped during the day, and then he wouldn't sleep at night! She'd shrug in a what-can-I-do kind of way.

My stomach grumbled. "Yeah," I told Levy, "let's eat something."

The kitchen was dark too, Levy's highchair still dirty from lunchtime with yogurt and crumbs.

I opened the oven. It was empty. I looked in the fridge.

"Michal," I called, "what should we eat?"

There was ketchup, a head of cabbage, raw potatoes, a carton of milk.

She trudged into the kitchen and looked over my shoulder at the fridge, "Hmm, I wanted to make you dinner… but the fridge was empty. *Uch*, I should have gone shopping today, I was just so exhausted, I don't even know why. Let's see…" she paused to think, "Throw something together! Surprise me."

She sat on a kitchen chair and went back to her phone, "did you know Sara had a baby? And Kara and Akiva got engaged. It was obvious though, I knew they would."

The options were cereal—I lifted the milk and discovered there was barely enough for a bowl, so scratch that—and salami. I spied the package in the back of the fridge. It was leftover from Shabbos. I found bread, still a few slices left and not too hard. Then I set it up on plates: bread, ketchup, salami, still holding Levy in my other arm. He was staring as he absentmindedly played with my collar, still too tired to act his usual hyper self.

"Tada!" I put a plate in front of Michal and strapped Levy into his high chair. For him, I made a mini sandwich with no ketchup. That would be too messy. I wiped the mess from earlier with a paper towel and finally collapsed into a chair.

But I forgot mine and Michal's dinner was on the counter! Forcing myself to my feet, I washed my hands and brought the plates to the table.

Michal looked from her phone to the sandwiches and laughed.

"What?" I insisted after I took a bite. It was cold and quite dry but not *too* bad.

"Men!" She rolled her eyes and explained, "I ask you to make dinner and you make a salami sandwich."

"Given the limited options," I said through clenched teeth and added, "by the way, I can't just leave work early. It doesn't work like that."

"When did you leave work early?"

"Today!"

She looked at the time on her phone, "pfft, barely."

"Well, it's a big deal for me." I'd have to go over all the notes from the meeting tomorrow morning and it still wouldn't be the same.

"You know what's a big deal for me?" Michal asked casually. She answered herself, "Taking care of this house every day of my life! So the next time I ask you to come home early, please consider doing as I ask."

"I did come home early," I said, my teeth still clenched, "besides, you said Levy was sleeping for hours. You didn't even need me home."

Michal folded her arms, "it's the principle."

"What principle?"

"You can help out here too, okay? Just because I'm a woman doesn't mean I have to be a slave to this house."

"Did I ever say you were?"

"It's kind of *implied* when you disappear for hours every day and then ask right when you get home, 'what's for dinner?' How should I know? Make your own dinner!"

I lifted my sandwich to take a bite. A glob of ketchup dripped onto the plate.

"You know what," I said, too tired to even argue, "let's just order take-out from now on."

Michal smiled and I sighed in relief. The one thing more stressful than leaving work early was a stressed-out wife.

Levy and I stayed up half the night together.

The next morning, when I left for work with my tall cup of coffee, he and Michal still slept peacefully.

On Vacation

We stepped from the terminal into the beating sun, squinting as we tracked down our cab. A minute in the open air and already, my *tzitzis* stuck to my skin. Beads of sweat dripped from my face down to my heavy leather shoes. I glanced at Mindy. She mustn't have been faring well either in her heavy wig, pantyhose and sleeveless dress worn over a long-sleeve shell.

We flew out from JFK barely three hours ago and now stepped off the plane into a different world. Back in New

York, they had already drawn into autumn, the leaves crisp and the winds harsh. All huddled in jackets, heads down against the grey skies. The season affected the mood too, honking horns just a little too long in the impossible back-to-school traffic.

Meanwhile, Miami remained oblivious. The palm trees swayed their gentle sway. We watched from the windows of our smooth car ride from Fort Lauderdale to Miami Beach. And everyone, from the cab driver to the locals smoking outside their shops—they all had a sun-kissed glow that gloated of lazy hours at the poolside.

This little getaway was quite spontaneous. Just two weeks ago, Mindy's father called and said his temporary tenants in Miami were leaving. It would be at least a month before they found new tenants. Would we want to spend some time in the house? It was fully furnished. The cleaning crew would have it ready for us by Sunday. I called my boss immediately.

"It's time you took some time off with your *kallah*," my boss started slowly, "I'll tell you what, I'll give you one week. Just bring your work laptop with you so you could do a few hours every day."

Yes, yes, yes. Within ten minutes the tickets were booked and we were set.

"You never went to Miami?" Mindy said when she found out, "How is that possible?"

"It never came up."

"What do you mean? So where did you go for mid-winter vacation?"

I shrugged, "my yeshiva didn't really have—"

"Pesach then? Summertime? Well, maybe it's too hot in the summer."

"We'd go to the country."

But now I was here, in the humid heat, with Mindy, my wife of half a year. I reached across the seat to squeeze her hand. She squeezed back and smiled.

We got to the house and began to unpack. I looked around at the spacious rooms, triple the size of our apartment in Brooklyn. Mindy was unloading the pots and pans from another duffel bag. The renters before us were Jewish and kept a kosher kitchen, our father-in-law ensured us, and the kitchen was fully stocked with pots and dishes. But Mindy and I decided not to trust the kitchen. Who knew who those tenants were? They could be a modern family for all we knew, with a flexible definition of the laws of kashrus. Better to be safe than sorry.

Mindy switched the air conditioner on, but even at full blast, sweat dripped down my brow. She unclipped the wig from her head and carefully brushed it through. Her wig was mid-length and muted blond. It used to be longer, like her own hair. But a month after she'd bought it, she'd frowned and said, "It doesn't feel right. I'm wearing this beautiful wig in an expression of what? *Modesty*?"

I was surprised at the drastic cut, but also proud, "you did the right thing," I told her, "and you know what? Now you're even more beautiful to me."

Mindy's hair underneath her wig was platinum blond, freshly dyed this month. She let it loose now. It fell nearly to her waist.

Modesty is a beautiful thing, I mused, but there are other beautiful things as well. I watched as Mindy, with her loose flowing hair, unpacked her clothes and changed out of her dress.

She turned back, "are you getting ready? I wanna get to the beach while the sun is still strong."

I looked down. I was wearing the same white shirt and black pants I wore every day, through scorching summers and freezing winters. I was ready to go anywhere. My feet did feel damp with sweat though. Perhaps I should change into my crocks even though I usually only wore them indoors.

As I wriggled out of my sweaty socks, Mindy went to the bathroom. A moment later she came out a changed woman. If I stared before—now I gaped.

"M-Mindy," I stuttered.

"Do you like?" She did a little twirl for me.

My cheeks flamed red down to my neck, whether from the heat or from Mindy's white bikini. The top consisted of two triangles, connected by a small string, very... exposing of the chest area. The bikini bottom was also made of just a triangle and a set of strings.

Six months, Mindy and I have had very intimate encounters... but not like this, in broad daylight!

"It's very well," I coughed, "very nice."

"Okay," she waited, "so let's go. You have your bathing suit in a bag or something?"

"What, where?"

"To the beach," she said impatiently, "it's just a five-minute walk. You should change here."

"Go where? *This*," I gestured in her general direction, "is for under your *shvimkleid*?" That's what all the women in my bungalow colony wore, not that I noticed. I always tried averting my eyes.

91

"What?" She laughed, "no, for under this." She picked up a sheer robe and tied it closed around her waist. With the long blond hair and her precious body exposed through the thin fabric, my wife looked like one of those women on the covers of magazines—again, not something I generally sought to see.

"Honey," I said hesitantly, "I don't think this is how a *bas Yisroel* dresses."

It was as glaringly clear as her bare shoulders and long exposed legs. I tried to pull my eyes away but couldn't. This was my Mindy? Basically naked and planning to go *outside*?

She laughed. Her laugh had me frozen. She looked like a supermodel (how I assumed supermodels looked, that is.) "We're on vacation!" she exclaimed, "relax a little," she reached over and unbuttoned my top buttons. I was dizzy from her touch.

"We'll buy you some t-shirts," she looked down at my feet, "and flip flops. Now come on."

"You're going out like this?" I said one last time, my feeble protest as she led the way to the door.

"What's the problem?" she shook her head, "who's here? Just *goyim* and out-of-towners"

I mumbled a *perek* of *Tehillim* under my breath, begging Hashem to forgive my immodest wife and my immodest thoughts.

"Oh," she paused at the door, "I forgot to cover my hair."

She disappeared inside for a second, reemerging with a straw hat perched atop her long flowing hair.

Just one week, I consoled Hashem and also myself. One short week. My stomach twisted into knots as I locked the door behind us.

In the Name of Love

It was an hour to Shabbos and we still had a twenty minutes' drive ahead of us. We were heading to Nachum's parents and were running late. Nachum hated it when we ran late, but the only person who hated it more was his mother.

"I expect you here two hours before *shkiah* at least!" she'd said on the phone yesterday.

"That's not possible," Nachum calmly explained, "I work until two."

What he didn't tell his mother was that we also enjoyed spending our Fridays leisurely and stress-free. When Nachum got home from work, we ate a long lunch of muesli with fresh fruits, did a work-out together—Nachum had no patience for yoga so I'd think of a good cardio-toning routine. Then we'd shower, choose our stuff for the weekend, pack up the car and finally, close to *shkiyah* and a half-hour drive ahead of us, we'd set off.

"Can you call my mom?" Nachum said as he turned onto the freeway, "tell her we're on the way."

"Sure," I put my lipstick away, applying it in the car wasn't the best idea anyway, and took his phone from the dashboard.

I called 'Mom' and held the phone to my ear.

Nachum's father picked up, and said warmly on the line, "Nachum!"

"No," I laughed, "it's just me, Ariella."

"Ariella! So nice of you to call."

"Yeah..." I hesitated and forced myself to say it: "is the missus around?"

"Who?"

I laughed again, more desperately now. Flustered. I had dialed Mom. Not Dad—MOM! Why was Nachum's father picking up the phone?

"Umm," What could I say? Let me speak to your wife? Too formal. So awkward. "We're on the way! Just let everyone know."

We bid our goodbyes and I adjusted the GPS back in place.

"You told her?" Nachum asked. Thankfully his eyes were on the road so they couldn't see my pink cheeks.

"Yeah, of course."

It was a problem. A big problem. A *huge* problem. The biggest of problems one can actually face in a relationship. The sort of problem that haunts you at every family gathering, damning you to a life of awkward encounters.

And worst still, this problem was too late to fix. Maybe I could have addressed it a month into our marriage. I even remember contemplating two months in if I should bring it up but I thought it was already too late. *Ha!* I should have said something. Now, one year and two months into our marriage, it was *really* too late.

I didn't know what to call my in-laws.

What Nachum calls them? Mom? Tatty? No way! The only Mom I had was the one who carried me in her womb. And *Tatty*? I'm just not the Yiddish type. Those words don't come to me naturally. I called my own father Dad, and again, it's reserved for the man who conceived and raised me. Not these random parents—sorry Nachum.

Mr. and Mrs. Leiberman? Oh gosh, I cringed at the thought.

Baruch and Malky? I pictured myself saying it countless times, even practiced to myself in my head. My sister's husband calls my parents by their names, why can't I? But Nachum's parents are *so* not the type. Their family is so weird about these things. Nachum doesn't even call his aunt and uncle by their proper name without an intro of Auntie or Uncle.

I cringed. I shuddered. My cheeks turned pink and I did what I always did when faced with this problem—I shoved it to the back of my mind and prayed to Hashem that everything would be fine.

And it was!

The drive was okay. Nachum's mom wasn't *too* stressed out when we arrived so close to candle lighting ("You should have told me you were on the way. I almost thought you wouldn't make it and you'd have to spend Shabbos on the side of the road!") Chezky, my little kiddo brother-in-law showed us to our room—as if Nachum didn't know where his old bedroom (now turned guest room) was.

But Chezky was just excited to see his big brother, badgering him with questions like, "did you ever beat the last round on Pokémon?" And, "you have to check out my new chess set!"

And before we knew it, we were all seated around to Shabbos table, heads still ringing with the tunes of *Kabbalas Shabbos*.

I was so relaxed, I almost let my guard down. Nachum was in the bathroom. Mrs... whatever, Nachum's mom was plating chicken in the kitchen with his two sisters which meant the salad course was almost over. I wanted a bit more of that cabbage salad before we switched courses so I looked around the table. And of course, it was next to Nachum's dad at the opposite end.

I cleared my throat and said in a loud and confident tone, "Can you pass the salad?"

Exactly then, my father-in-law broke out into song. "*Teee ly ly ly, tee ly ly ly.*"

I bit my finger and tried one more time, "Can you please pass it? The cabbage salad."

Chesky looked up, "What do you need?"

"Just want to try that salad," I pointed.

"Oh, just speak up. Ta, can you pass the salad over?"

I didn't even taste the cabbage, my cheeks were so red.

"This is a really pretty necklace, where's it from?" Rachelli, my eighteen-year-old sister-in-law asked. Shabbos afternoon, we were sitting in the living room, schmoozing about life and dating. She was wondering if she should start because all of her friends already spoke to *shadchanim*. I told her it's important for her to feel ready. I was a big advocate of *not* rushing, as I myself only started dating at nineteen.

I drew my hands to the gold heart pendant on my necklace and said, "You don't know?"

"How would I know?"

I looked up. My mother-in-law was on the couch across from us. She looked up when she heard the word *'necklace'* and smiled.

"It was a really nice gift from a very special person," I winked at my mother-in-law to answer her expectant look and Rachelli's question.

Rachelli was focused on her nails. She didn't see, "It's from Nachum?"

"No! It's from your mom."

Is that appropriate to say? *Your* mom in the presence of said mom. Neither my mother-in-law nor Rachelli looked aghast so I hoped it was fine.

Uch. Why didn't these parents go to sleep on Shabbos afternoon like normal parents? Why did they insist on *'spending time with the kids?'*

There was one more incident that actually caused me retire to my room to rest. I couldn't take it anymore. Way too much stress in this house.

We were playing a game. The whole family! Is that normal? All the kids, parents and all?

Chaya, the eleven-year-old sister made it up. It was called *Most Likely To* and we had to pick notes from the jar.

Did you make this game specifically for Shabbos afternoon? I wanted to ask so badly but I held myself back.

"Most likely to win a chess tournament?"

Everyone but Nachum agreed on Chezky. "But I beat Chezky!" Nachum protested.

"Most likely to own a clothing store?"

Me. It was unanimous. I'm happy they appreciate my style around here.

"Most likely to open a restaurant?"

Mom. Mom. Mom. I didn't say anything.

"What do *you* think?" Chezky asked and everyone's eyes turned to me.

"Rachelli," I said and laughed. Okay, so it was way more my mother-in-law's type but I could see Rachelli running a restaurant too.

"Me?" she shrieked, "it's so not my type! It's way more Mom's type."

I looked at my mother-in-law, laughing, "Oh yeah, it is *your* type."

Nachum came into the room to wake me up for *Havdalah*. I'd been reading the *Mishpacha* magazine while reveling in my solitude.

"Will you stay to play Wii with us?" Chezky asked after *Havdalah*.

"No, we're in a rush. We have a long drive ahead," I said before Nachum could answer.

We were packed in minutes, bidding farewells and finally in the safety of our car with the comfort of having done my monthly duty of Shabbos at the in-laws. *Baruch Hashem* for that.

"I just don't get it," Nachum said as we drove down the road, "I don't get why you don't like being by my parents."

His voice was so forlorn, my heart hurt a little bit.

"Of course I love it there! Your family is amazing, they're so sweet! It's just overwhelming for me. I'm not used to so much... happening."

"You have eight siblings."

"Well, we're different."

Nachum looked over at me uncertainly.

"Really," I insisted, "I love your parents."

I just wish I knew what to call them...

Mixed Dancing

The dim garden lights complimented Yael's subtle features, big eyes and long *sheitel*. She looked beautiful and I told her so. We were at Café Rimon, seated outdoors, the early summer breeze cooling our skin. Motzei Shabbos was our thing. It was our set date night since we got married a little over six months ago. Our married friends had smiled ironically and said, *good luck keeping it up*. But we were still going strong.

"Less than a month to Mikey's wedding," I grinned just as our waiter left with our order. Mikey was my older brother, twenty-seven and the best guy ever. He met his fiancé Nava in the Philippines on a trip after university. It's been three years and he finally popped the question much to my parent's relief. It's one thing having a son *off-the-derech*. It's another having him live in Tel Aviv with a woman that was not his wife.

Yael mirrored my smile and spoke about two other wedding invites we had for the upcoming month, what she'd wear, who we'd see.

It was only when our food came—a salad for her, a pasta for me—and she picked at the vegetables grudgingly that she said, "How can you be so close to someone that does the things he does?"

"Hey," I dropped my fork back into my bowl, suddenly defensive, "Mikey's a good guy. He doesn't do anything wrong."

Yael looked up at me and after a laden pause she said, "So not keeping Shabbos is okay?"

I rolled my eyes, "You know what I mean."

"No, I don't know what you mean." She said stubbornly, "Explain."

"You know Mikey, I don't have to explain," I said, equally as stubborn.

"I bet the wedding won't even be kosher," she examined her nails as she spoke.

"Don't be ridiculous," I said, "Besides, my parents are paying half and you know they wouldn't let anything less than *Badatz.*"

"So how could they let mixed seating?"

I didn't answer back, focusing on my meal instead. Hyper-intense chewing. I had enough of this.

Yael had not. She continued, "You know, I'm betting there will be mixed dancing as well. Mikey is going to embarrass your parents. Don't you care? I don't get it. Why can't you stand up for anything?"

"Are you serious?" I sputtered, "it's Mikey's wedding. He's a big boy and he can make his own decisions."

"And you're his closest brother," Yael hissed back, "don't you think it's your place to tell him something? Because *clearly,* no one else will."

"What should I say? Don't dance like that? Don't eat like that? Don't have *your* wedding with the woman *you* love the way *you* want 'cause your little brother said so?" I laughed humorlessly at the thought of it.

"If you know he's doing wrong in Hashem's name, I don't see why not." She folded her arms and looked away, at the other tables, at her salad, at her phone, everywhere but me.

She added, "and not because you said so. It's because it's the wrong thing to do. He's doing the wrong thing."

"It's between him and *Hashem*."

"And all the hundreds of people that will be there! You think mixed dancing doesn't affect their *neshama*? Why don't you do it then?"

An elderly couple from the table closest peered at us curiously. They hastily looked away when I caught their stares.

"Yael…" I said slowly.

"Don't *Yael* me." she snapped, "you were always so reasonable. Always stood up for what's right. Remember when we were dating, when we went for coffee and they only charged you for one cup? You went all the way back after our date to pay for the second cup. *That's* how I knew you were for me. You did the right thing. But now it's a much bigger deal and you're staying quiet. I'm sorry if you don't want to hear all this, but if I don't say it, who will?"

That week I called Mikey.

"Bro, I haven't spoken to you in days, how's your little lady?"

As nervous as I was, I couldn't help the smile spread across my face. Mikey's enthusiasm was infectious, "Yael is great! She just started a new job in sales. It's not such a big shot company, but there's lots of room for growth."

"Ambitious, that one," Mikey laughed.

"And you? How's Nava? Is she going bridezilla on you?"

"Nah, you know how we are, both super chilled. Like, we just want to have an awesome night, y'know? No drama. Just lots of love and music."

"Oh yeah," I said as if I just remembered, "You spoke to Ima about the band? She's picky with that stuff..." I trailed off.

"Nah, she's cool with it. We're having a DJ. I spoke to the 'rents, I told them, like, don't get involved, just let me have my night. They get it. They really do. It's amazing actually, I feel like it's the first in a long time that we can actually talk."

"That's—that's great! But, Abba's also okay with it? The dancing and all?"

"I don't know man, it's weird," Mikey's content sigh rose static on the line, "For once they're accepting me as I am. They're not judging."

"I'm happy for you, really," I said. And I was. I just wasn't happy for myself; how the heck was I going to tell Yael I didn't confront my brother?

"What can I do?"

It was evening and Yael said she needed a bath. That was forty-five minutes ago and the door was firmly locked. All I told her was that Mikey would have his wedding his way. That I wouldn't get involved.

I knocked on the door again and called, "What do you want me to do, Yael? What can I do?"

No answer.

I gave up, laid down on my bed catching up on my Whatsapps and watching all the funny or inspirational videos sent my way.

Finally, Yael emerged in PJ's, her hair dripping, her expression dire. She slipped into her bed, dragging her blanket to her neck. Tonight our beds were separate, the foot of space between our mattresses expanded like miles. It was the hardest time of the month and now more than ever I wanted to hold her tight.

She didn't speak until she was completely settled, and only then in a chilling whisper, "*Al ta'amod al dam rei'echa.*"

She turned over, her back to me. Her words hung in the air. The passage from the Torah that commands not to stand by idly as your friend bleeds.

"Ima," I started awkwardly, "you don't think it's going to be a bit... much for Abba—the music, the dancing?"

My mother sighed heavily from her end of the line, "what can I do? What can I do?" she said eventually, "This is my *bochur*. He's going to do things his way, he always has, whether we're involved or not."

"But..." each word was painful, my conscious begging me to be quiet for Mikey's sake, I extracted them painfully from my throat, "there's going to be a lot of *halachic* issues. It's one thing to be a guest... it's another to host such an event."

"Oh, don't I know it," my mother said and then weird breathing from her end. It took me a moment to realize she was crying.

"Ima! I'm sorry, I shouldn't get involved."

"You are so right—" she paused to sniffle, "you don't have kids yet, *neshamale*, but once you do, you'll understand. I just want a connection with my dear Michael."

She was the only one that called Mikey that. I said I'm sorry again, offered some consoling words and assured her she was a strong woman and that she was doing the right thing.

"You're a good boy," she said, "thank you."

"I'm going to dry clean my suit," I announced, pulling it out of the closet on the hanger. It was a casual comment, but I said it a bit too loudly, a bit too deliberately for it to be completely harmless.

"For what?" Yael blinked her big eyes.

"Thursday night," she didn't react, "the wedding," I added.

"Why? You barely need a suit for a wedding like that," she folded the freshly laundered towels carefully into a pile.

"I like to look presentable."

"Well," she shrugged, "I don't have a dress."

"We still have a week until the wedding. We can drive to Bnei Barack and find something." I scooped up the towels to bring them to the closet.

"No," she said with half a smile, "I don't have a dress because I'm not going."

I halted in my tracks, "really?"

"No one in your family is saying anything and honestly, I am both disgusted and shocked. So I am going to act. You can tell them I'm not feeling well or something." She said it offhandedly as if she were discussing a trip to the mall.

"I'm not leaving you here alone."

"And I'm not letting you celebrate in a way you don't believe in… in a way you are so against!" she jumped up and stormed past me, stopping at the door, "Sometimes I feel like I don't even know who you are anymore. Definitely not the man I married."

She turned on her heel and slammed the door after her.

I groaned and fell back onto my bed, wondering where the kind, accepting woman *I* married had gone. The image of her face twisted in disgust imprinted on my mind.

"That's tough," Gavi said thoughtfully.

Gavi was the guy from my *chevre* I trusted most with these things. He and his wife were together for three years and had two perfect babies in that time, *bli ayin hara*. They were the happiest couple I knew. So it only made sense, that in my growing desperation, I called him for advice.

"But what can you do?" he said, "She's the woman."

"He's my *brother*."

"Look, your family is important, but you *always* have to put your wife first. That's how it works. She's the most important thing now."

"So I should let her stay home?" and then I realized the only true option with growing horror, "*I should stay home with her?*"

"Look, man, I'm not gonna tell you what to do but I could tell you what I would do. Don't leave her alone for a second. Even if she says it's fine—she'll remember it forever."

Yael and I were together for half a year. Me and Mikey? Brothers for 23, my whole *entire* life.

I was relieved for Yael's sake that it was early afternoon. Another five hours to calm down until I had to see her again.

Thursday night, the weather was perfect, hot but not unbearable like weather can be in July. The moon was bright, smiling. The stars were out. I stood on the balcony, staring up at them. Right around now Nava and Mikey would be standing under the *chuppah*, under this same sky, my parents beside him, my four little siblings seated up front. Grandparents, cousins, friends... And all this was taking place some forty-five minutes from here in a charming garden hall.

My phone buzzed in my hand. From Gavi: *You're doing the right thing.*

Another buzz: a family photo fresh on our family chat, everyone done-up and smiling. My little sister Chaya sent it, followed by another one. Mikey and the guys. And another, the whole family. I was glaringly missing. I silenced the phone and squeezed it until my knuckles turned white.

"You know you can go if you want," Yael had told me an hour ago, already in pajamas, cooking popcorn on the stove, "I don't want to stop you..."

And I had wanted to yell at her. I had wanted to scream at her—to do something, *anything* to hurt her. To watch her face crumble. *That manipulative*—no. Deep breath.

"It's okay darling," I had smiled, "I'm staying right here with you."

Victory Spoils

I came home too late, grumpy and stressed, the big house looming over me. Our garden was out of hand. My shadows bounced off of the overgrown shrubs as I crossed the path from the driveway to the front door. The gardener was supposed to come today. I pulled out my phone and wrote out a reminder to call him.

I let myself in through the heavy mahogany door. Glancing at my reflection as I hung my jacket in the coat closet. It was a full-length mirror hiding on the inside of the closet door. I always forgot about it, and then, when I'd open the door to hang my jacket, it would sneak up on me, never failing to disappoint.

My eyes. When did they get so hollow and tired? And when did my mouth turn down in that serious way? Was I imagining the downward lines imprinted at their corners? I was thirty-one, not forty!

But I dressed like a forty-year-old in a blazer and suit skirt, low heels and sheer pantyhose. I fluffed my hair, smiled to show off my teeth and hide the lines, and shut the closet door.

Then I went inside.

"I'm home!" I called. But the living room was dark, opening into the dining room—dark too. The only light emitted from the top of the staircase, accompanied by some distant laughter and the running water.

I sighed and flipped the lights on. Ezra was always doing that—turning them off to shave a few dollars off the electric bill. Well, I'd rather come home with all of our crystal lights lit.

Another peel of laughter echoed from upstairs. The water was off now. I heard more clearly. The deeper male voice and two squeaks of our girls.

"Ezra!" I leaned on the banister and yelled upstairs.

"Mommy's home!" I heard him say and the girls shrieked in laughter again.

"Mommy, Mommy, Mommy," he ran down the staircase, the girls trailing after him. Maya was too slow. He scooped her little towel-clad body in his arms and hopped down the steps.

"Mommy," he put Maya down and gave me a quick peck, "we just finished with bath time."

"Wanna kiss Mommy too!" Maya pouted. She was almost four years old and positively darling with huge eyes and golden hair.

I stooped to give her a tight hug. Her hair made my shoulder damp. I pulled back and waved at Bella, seven years old and standing back, also in a towel, giggling at something Ezra had said.

"Mommy had a long day," I said suddenly exhausted at the attention and the pain that accompanied it, "she is very tired. And hungry."

"Did you hear that?" Ezra took Maya's hand, "Mommy's hungry! Let's show her what we made."

Bella ran to take Ezra's free hand, holding her towel up with the other.

I followed them to the kitchen. The marble countertops were spotless except for two trays.

"I wanna show her," Bella said to her father, "I designed them best."

"Go ahead," he kicked the stool towards her, which she pointedly ignored, "look," she reached and threw the foil off of one tray, "I made the purple and blue cookies. The flower is for Maya, the heart is for Daddy, the star is for me and the circle is for you."

"I made you cookies too!" Maya jumped up and down, her towel slipping.

"You girls are going to get in pajamas or what?"

"You didn't taste a cookie yet!" Maya pouted.

"Oh, of course." I nibbled the edge of the purple and blue circle, "delicious!"

"That's not dinner, don't worry," Ezra uncovered the round tray, "spinach quiche. I figured I'd crack open that cookbook your aunt got us. It has some awesome stuff."

"Oh, thank god," the dough was thick and there was still over half the quiche left.

I turned to the girls again, "pajamas?"

"Bella, are you going to tell your mother about your spelling test first?"

"Mommy doesn't care." She shrugged and turned to go upstairs.

"That is not true!" I snapped, "Tell me about it."

"I got an 87," she said, looking down.

"Well, that's okay. You studied?"

"You see!" Bella turned and ran up to her room. At Ezra's stern eyes, Maya reluctantly followed.

"She's just a bit sensitive," Ezra told me as we sat with warmed up quiche. Only a slice for him because he ate before and a huge chunk for me, I was starved, "She's not so great with spelling. Her teacher said we should get her tested for dyslexia. She studied for hours for that test."

"Dyslexia?" I looked down at my steaming plate. Dyslexia sounded as foreign as another language. "Why didn't you tell me?"

"I only heard at the parents-teachers meeting on Monday."

"And I asked you how it went. You didn't say that."

"No, you said, 'are the teachers proud?' and you didn't wait to hear my answer."

"Are you saying I'm a bad mother?" I stabbed my quiche and Ezra flinched.

"I never said that. Stop taking her dyslexia personally. Just... just be proud of her, even if she doesn't get great grades."

"I'm always proud of Bella," I said quietly. Bella's intelligent eyes and sly humor. Her creativity and sense of authority.

"Then act more like it."

I went to Bella's room. She was hiding in her princess canopy bed, drawing pictures on her tablet.

I flipped on her fairy lights and she looked up, her eyes widening slightly.

"Why are you in my room?" she didn't say it harshly, but not softly either.

"I always say *shema* with you," I stood awkwardly between the door and her bed.

"No, you *sometimes* say *shema* with me. Sometimes you're busy and you forget." This girl was too observant for her own good.

"Well, tonight I didn't forget," I sat on her bed under the tulle of the canopy, "I also wanted to say congratulations on your test. I'm so proud of you."

"Daddy told you to say that," she said, at least she smiled though, "I heard."

"And I am *not* proud of you for eavesdropping!"

The rest of the week passed painstakingly slowly until finally, finally, I left the office late Friday with a thousand things already piled on my desk for Monday, and sped home to a sinking sun.

I barely had time to shower and wash my hair, throw on a dress and dab on some makeup. My alarm rang, telling me I took too much time. I shut my phone off and bound downstairs to light the candles.

Finally, finally—with the two flames lit, transforming the house from every day to Shabbat—I could breathe. Outside, the sun still set, but less urgently now.

"Mommy," Maya pulled my dress, "read me a story."

"Your mother is exhausted," Ezra pulled her away and put a hand around my waist, "you look dead on your feet. Don't worry, I've got them. I'll take them to *shul*. They'll play with the Rosenberg girls."

"Thank you," I said and felt it in every nerve in my body. Relaxed.

We ate dinner—a combination of Ezra's experimental cooking and store-bought trays. That's what I reached for— the organic chicken, sautéed string beans, and olive tapenade from the store.

Maya spoke about kindergarten. Her best friend Sarah, who didn't want to share crayons with her.

"I don't know if she's my best friend anymore," she said sadly.

"Don't worry," Ezra told her, "I think you should talk to her and explain how you feel. Maybe she'll let you use them next time. But remember, you're not her friend for her crayons, are you?"

Bella rolled her eyes, bored, "who cares? Maya always fights with Sarah! What's for dessert?"

"I brought something," I piped up. It was easy to fall into a sleepy state, just observing. Ezra was *so* good with them. He always knew what to say. I was in awe and, I didn't want to admit, slightly jealous. They just responded to him differently... friendlier.

"You?" Bella's face twisted in doubt, "You don't bake."

"I go to the store." I said, "Sometimes."

"No, you don't."

I wasn't going to fight with a seven-year-old, especially one who noticed too much, "one of my employees brought it in. It was his birthday so his wife made the most perfect cupcakes. They were so good, I saved some so you could taste."

"I want, I want, I want!" Maya said, "Cupcakes!"

"You didn't finish your chicken," Ezra pushed her plate back towards her.

Bella didn't say anything.

We ate Shabbat lunch late and went for a short walk in the neighborhood. The sun was strong and the wind was mild. I rolled up my sleeves and tilted my face upward to soak it all in.

"I think we could open the pool this week," Ezra said. He wore short sleeves and Ray-bans. Maya and Bella ran ahead. They impatiently waited at the crosswalk.

"If you can't be on top of the garden, how could you be on top of the pool?"

"What's wrong with the garden?"

"I spoke to the gardener. He told me you never even called him to come. I can't take care of *everything*."

"I didn't realize it was a problem."

"That's what I'm afraid of. The pool will be filthy with leaves and bugs before you *realize* you need to call someone to clean it. And do you even have the number for the girls' swimming instructor, or will I have to find that too?"

"I said I'll take care of it."

"I'll believe it when I see it."

At home, I looked out the floor to ceiling window of our bedroom. The pool was covered with a thick tarp. It would be nice to open it up, if just for the view.

I shook my head, too much to think about. It was Shabbat, still early afternoon. I had to rest instead of wasting time worrying. I went to bed with a book, barely got through a page and fell fast asleep.

By the time I opened my eyes again, it was dark. The view out the window showed a colorful sky with the last fading rays of sunshine. What time was it? Where was Ezra? His bed was still made. He hadn't napped at all today.

I jumped up, fastened a robe and went downstairs.

They were in the dining room. I heard them all the way up the stairs. Bella's indignant cries of, "it's not fair! Daddy, she's taking *so* long."

Ezra and the girls were around the dining room table, Rummikub tiles spread across the wood.

"Why didn't you wake me?" I grumbled, wiping sleep away from my eyes.

Ezra looked up, "Hi honey, we didn't want to bother you. Maya, you're taking too long. Bella, what do you want me to do, she doesn't know the rules..."

"Yes I do," Maya put her last tile in her mouth and said a muffled, "I won!"

"Did you rest well? God knows you needed it. Don't worry, I took care of the girls, right girls?"

"Daddy! We're in the middle of a game! It's your turn, go," Bella huffed.

"Of course, thank you. That's very considerate of you, Ezra," but I couldn't stick around to watch them play. My throat was clogged with I don't know what—feelings I've been swallowing for too long. When did I start to feel like this? To feel like I've become an observer in my own home.

I usually worked on Sundays, from my office at home. No travel, fewer hours. Still, it helped a lot, getting a head start on the workload. Today, I couldn't focus. I started at six a.m., sat for a half-hour with my morning coffee, but my mind was on blank so I changed into sneakers and went for a jog.

Shabbat usually left me invigorated. Well, recently it's been leaving me restless. But now, I felt neither invigorated nor restless, just sad.

Now, half an hour into my jog, sweat dripping from my forehead, and legs tight from strain, I didn't feel any better. I took a route through the nature center, past endless trees.

Quiet. Beautiful. Empty at seven A.M. It's what I loved about this little town. In the open nature, yet still somehow, impossibly, a half-hour away from the ever-bustling Manhattan.

Here, we were able to buy a big house, with a big pool. Nice neighbors, but far enough so we'd still have privacy— something impossible to come by in the city. And I was still able to work in the city. Back and forth from Manhattan every day, the commute drove me crazy... but it gave me time to think.

Ezra worked ten minutes away, at a small New Jersey firm. We were both lawyers. At the start of our careers, newlywed and ambitious, I'd told him, "I want it all. I want a lot of kids. A lot of money. I want to be successful. Can I have it all?"

"It's either me or you," Ezra said heavily, "I also want a career."

"So what do you want to do? What every man does? Steal the glory while I cook dinner and clean the floors?"

"First of all," he said firmly, "neither of us is ever going to be cleaning floors. We shouldn't take away work from the cleaning people, should we?"

I laughed, "no, of course not. How will our economy survive?"

"Second," he sighed, "we'll both work hard and reevaluate what we want when we have kids."

By the time Bella was born, I already started my Manhattan job. It paid over double Ezra's. The decision was made for us. He shortened his hours, I got another raise, more responsibilities on my shoulders.

On days like today, I wondered, what if it had been different? What if I'd gotten the job in New Jersey, giving legal advice to homeowners? A nice $150,000 a year like Ezra, I would have felt accomplished enough.

That lump in my throat—it came back again, clogging it, making it hard to breathe. I walked the rest of the way home.

The girls were at gymnastic practice, Ezra was in the basement building a wooden bench. He had been working on it for a few weeks now but he wasn't very good at it. Screws poked out and one leg was too short. It was cute though—the way his face scrunched in concentration behind his safety glasses, his hair speckled with wood chips.

He noticed me watching and took his glasses and earmuffs off, "what do you think? I think I'll get it done today. I just have to sand and paint it."

"Is there anything you can do about the screws?"

"Hmm, I'll check online."

We stood together, admiring his okay handiwork. It was a complex project, legs crossed in an X shape.

"Ezra," I put a hand on his arm, "look what's happening to me."

"What?"

I did it again, I made this about me. But I was too emotional to care, "why did you let me do it?"

"Do *what*? Speak."

"Work so hard. You're a man. You're supposed to tell me to take it easy, tell me you'll take care of me. Instead, I work sixty hours a week and barely know my own daughters. Do you see the way Bella looks at me sometimes?"

"Why don't I tell you to take it easy?" he said, "I cannot believe you, of all people, are saying that!"

"What, why?" it didn't escape my notice that he completely ignored the second part of what I said.

"You're saying that *I*, as a *man* should take care of *you*, a *woman*? Say it again, I need a video of this or no one will believe me."

"Stop it," I folded my arms and backed away to the wall, "you know this isn't fair."

127

"What?" he raised his voice, "that you get to work the job of your dreams while I waste away in a rando firm in *NEW JERSEY*? I did this all for you so don't give me that!"

"Sure seems like it," I scoffed, "you must have it *so* bad, having all the time in the world, time with your two kids that adore you, time to try out new recipes, and now all the money in the world as well! You are set, now that your sugar mama takes care of you."

"Do you hear what you're saying?"

"Loud and clear"

"What happened to equality? Or is that just talk?"

"Some equality this is! I work my ass off for this home. And you? You have fun with Maya and Bella."

"So quit," he kicked his bench, "go for it! You can be the mom you want to be. I'm not stopping you. Do what you want. You always did."

"You are unbelievable."

"*Me?*" he opened his mouth and then shut it again. Smart man. He at least knew when to shut up.

"You're stressed," Ezra said next week, "It's almost Memorial Day weekend. Let's fly to the Bahamas. We could fly out of Newark on Thursday and be back Monday night."

"Very cute," I nodded, "I'm stressed so you're planning a trip with the money *I* make and you're not even taking my work schedule into account. I can't skip Friday, even on a holiday weekend."

"So what do *you* want to do?"

"Try out a new recipe, go to a yoga class, maybe go shopping at the mall? What do you and all the other moms in this dumb town ever do?"

"Okay, then I'll ask the girls if they want to come with *me* to the Bahamas. With the money I earn. You're forgetting, aren't you? That I still go to work and make a nice paycheck?"

That was the first night of many that I slept on the couch. It was too much. This big house was too much. Bella's scorn was too much and Maya's undeserved affection was almost worse. Handsome, smart, earnest Ezra was definitely too much.

I closed my eyes and pictured it all differently. Longingly.

Baby, One More Time

"What's that noise?" I opened my bleary eyes.

"Oh, I'm sorry—shhh," my wife held the baby, Chaya Rina, tight to her chest, lulling her gently as she lifted her shirt to nurse her. Chaya Rina's sobs slowly subsided.

I rolled over and just as easily fell back asleep.

"I think it's too much," Dini announced.

"What is?" I looked up from the daily shiur I received on Whatsapp as I ate eggs on toast. Dini was breastfeeding Chaya Rina while hand-feeding Bassy in the high chair. Chaya Rina, tangled in fabric, starting crying. Bassy gleefully tossed little bits of egg onto the floor.

I smiled at the two little ones and then at my wife, always happy despite her lack of sleep—a true woman of valor—then I looked back at my *shiur*. If I didn't read through it by breakfast I had a tendency to skip it altogether.

"I think it's too much," Dini said again.

"I'm sorry," I looked up again, "what is?"

Dini placed a wailing Chaya Rina in her bassinet and looked at me. Her bottom lip quivered and her forehead wrinkled.

"This," she said vaguely, as if I was a mind reader, "everything."

Bassy sensed the change in her mother and grew agitated. She slapped the high chair table and sprayed egg bits all over the floor.

"I don't understand." I shook my head and quickly read the last few lines on my phone. It was a nice bit on *shalom bayis*, real practical tips. I'd have to forward it to my sister Shani, she and her husband always argued at the Shabbos table.

Dini sighed and started, "I'm exhausted—"

"Oh no," I stood up, "it's nearly eight." I gave Bassy a pat on the head and Dini a quick smile. I taught *Gemara* to fourth and fifth grade at a local yeshiva. I had to be there for the first class after *davening* at eight-thirty but I liked to get there early to chat with Rabbi Goldstein and Mr. Schechter in the teacher's room.

"We'll talk later?"

"Of course," I said, wondering what on earth we could discuss.

The day passed in a lazy blur. After teaching, I met with my *chavrusa* Yair to learn the *daf yomi*, then we sat for a bit and caught up. He told me he had started learning to play the guitar.

"My wife always insists I sing *Havdalah* so I'm going to surprise her and add instruments too!" he explained.

"That sounds awesome," I thought back to yeshiva days, I'd always admired Yossi, the one who could transform any *kumzitz* with his heavenly strumming. "Maybe I should also learn to play. I have plenty of free time now."

"There's no time like the present," Yair agreed and gave me the number of his excellent teacher.

By the time I got home after a lengthy *mincha*, the sun had nearly set. I hummed as I unlocked the front door.

My humming stopped abruptly. Both babies were screaming, the bath was on, and the house smelled faintly of cabbage. Dini knew I hated it when she added cabbage to the vegetable soup. It was going to be a long evening, I groaned.

Dini emerged, a baby in each hand, both in snug onesies with a towel around them. She let Bassy down to crawl on the floor.

We were married for two years and I've seen Dini in all sorts of states, having fathered two children and all... but I still wasn't completely used to having a woman around, especially one so... womanly. Usually, she was perfectly modest. But now her soaked dress was plastered to her chest outlining her body clearly.

"Your dress is wet," I said, my ears red.

"I hadn't noticed," Dini said crossly.

Her face ruined the picture. It was twisted into a frown with those wrinkles between her eyebrows.

"Cheer up," I said with a smile, "How was your day? You made cabbage soup." I said it as a statement so she could take it however she wanted. I wasn't putting her down or acting ungrateful, merely stating a fact so she could come to the realization on her own.

"I wanted cabbage soup," she said and shivered.

"You should change."

She handed me the baby and went to the room.

I held Chaya Rina and played with her little hands. Then tickled her neck and pulled funny faces. The baby didn't smile. If anything she squirmed uncomfortably in my arms. Bassy found a box of tissues and pulled them out one by one.

"Dini!" I called.

She didn't answer.

Chaya Rina started making this noise, not quite crying but almost. I tensed up and started rocking her like I'd seen Dini do and called my wife again.

Finally, Dini emerged in a dry robe.

"You left me with her for twenty minutes!" I said, thrusting the baby towards her.

Dini held Chaya Rina and in an instant she was calm.

I shook my head, the stress of the home already creeping under my skin. This is why I liked staying out and coming home late. Everywhere else my presence was validated. Here, everything I did somehow seemed wrong. Like this family got along fine without me. *My* family. I bet Dini even preferred me away. I sulked.

"What we were talking about in the morning..." Dini started.

I sighed, "Let's talk over food, please? It's been a long day, I can't think straight."

So Dini ladled two bowls of vegetable-cabbage soup and carefully brought them to the table. Just as we started eating, Chaya Rina whined. She was hungry too. Dini sighed and unzipped her robe. I looked down to pick the cabbage pieces from my bowl.

"I'm going on birth control," Dini announced once Chaya Rina was happily hidden in her dress.

I sputtered, my spoon of soup spraying Dini across the table.

She blinked and continued, "I called my doctor for a prescription. She said I could already pick it up tomorrow."

It took a moment for me to regain my voice, "what are you talking about Dini? What are you saying?"

"I told you already!" she exploded, "I'm exhausted and I just can't do it! I would *die* if I found out I was pregnant again. DIE. I am not ready."

"But—" I sputtered again, "but—but you can't! We still don't have a son. This is clearly a decision the two of us should be making together." it was true! My suspicions were right. Dini didn't even want me here. She wanted to make all the big decisions herself. I folded my arms and refused to look at her face.

"I gave birth twice in twenty months! I feel weak all the time. And tired. And fat and ugly. Like a cow!" she faltered, her voice dropping to a whisper, "I just want to feel like me." and she was crying, fat teardrops landing straight into her bowl of soup. Well, I thought wryly, it could use the extra salt.

"I think you're overreacting," I said slowly, "let's take a few months to think about this before making any rash decisions..."

Dini tensed up. She breathed deeply and I sensed another explosion coming.

"Anyways," I continued, "You said... you said you couldn't if you're still... feeding." My ears turned pink again. I couldn't say *breast*feeding. I just couldn't say it.

"I got pregnant with Chaya Rina when I was breastfeeding. You don't remember?" Dini sobbed. Chaya Rina, as if summoned, started crying again. Dini consoled her through her tears.

My head hurt, "this is very overwhelming for me and not something you can just decide on lightly." I took a deep breath, "I would speak to my Rabbi but it's so embarrassing. I know he'll say we should wait for a son." What would the

Rabbi think of my wife if I told him? Which good wife wouldn't complete the *mitzvah* of *Pru Urvu* for their husband? One daughter and one son, at the very least.

"I can't do it," Dini whispered.

But she was quiet and the tears were drying up.

I showered as she got the little ones into bed, already devising a plan in my head. She just couldn't take those horrid pills.

"Dini," I reached over to her once we were both in bed that night, "I'm going to speak it over with my Rabbi, see what he thinks, but for now... don't go and get them, okay?"

"You'll talk to him tomorrow?" she said.

"As soon as possible," I promised. That meant I could speak to him in a week and phrase the question a little differently, perhaps: *what does the Torah think about birth control?*

"As I said, I don't think we should start playing G-d now."

Dini started to protest, decided against it and just stared at the ceiling.

"Now, do you think we should..." I still had trouble initiating sex. It just didn't come to me naturally. But Dini understood my half-sentences by now. She accepted and we fulfilled our marital duties.

During the next few months, Dini would bring up the topic again, but not like she had that night. No tears, no yelling, just a simple, "I'm not sure I'm ready yet."

"Hashem will give us strength," I'd console her.

"Did you speak to the Rabbi yet?"

"He doesn't think it's the best option."

What he had said was something like, "I'd only suggest birth control if a wife can't mentally and physically handle it." My Dini can handle everything.

And then, not five months later, the answer to our prayers came in the form of Dini puking in the toilet bowl at six a.m. A pregnancy test confirmed it. She was pregnant! And despite her complaints, her eyes sparkled and I knew it was the right thing for us.

Eight months later we were blessed with a baby girl. Dini clutched the beautiful bundle in her arms as Chaya Rina cried for attention and Bassy pulled her skirt. We looked down at the perfect scrunched face and I whispered, "Next year, we'll be blessed with a *bris, b'ezras Hashem*"

Help Wanted

"We'll start this Sunday," Rivka said, pushing the shopping cart towards the vegetable aisle, "I'll call to make an appointment."

It was Thursday night and, as usual, we were on our weekly shopping trip.

I ran up to relieve her of the cart, "I just don't understand *why*. We're perfectly fine." This was an ongoing discussion between us, and thus far our only source of disagreement, "we got married two months ago, we're doing *Baruch Hashem* just fine, I feel like I could talk to you about anything... I just—I don't get why we need marriage *counseling.*"

"Stop saying it like that," Rivka said, pursing her lips as she examined a pepper for blemishes.

"Like what?"

"Like it's a bad thing! All this stigma around counseling and therapy..." she handed me a bag to collect cucumbers, "honestly, we should have started earlier."

"Earlier *when*?" I was stupefied. "It's been two months. Two *wonderful* months," I added.

"All my friends started right when they got engaged."

I laughed, and then realized she wasn't joking. "It's *marriage* counseling. There has to be some aspect of *marriage* to it, doesn't there?"

"You don't get it!" She took the cart and steered it towards the dairy section. "It's supposed to help us prepare and figure out how to communicate through things. Just like," she thought, "like parenting classes before you have kids."

"Don't tell me you want to do that too." I peeked at her sideways to catch her expression.

She shrugged and chose the freshest dated cottage cheese.

"Look, all my friends told me it's the best thing ever. It's just the thing to do. Literally *everyone* does it! *And*, it really helped their communication with their husbands, so isn't it worth it? If it just helps a teeny, tiny bit?"

"But we communicate just fine!"

"I know," she admitted quietly, "but, we really don't know how the rest of our marriage will be. Marriage is complicated. We're going to go through a lot together..."

"And if we feel like we *need* counseling," I continued for her, "we will go."

"No, no, no," she shook her head, "*everyone* does it before. We're late as it is."

"So what? Every couple is different, obviously. Maybe they have problems. *Baruch Hashem*, we don't... unless," I bit my finger as it dawned on me, "you do have a problem with me and you're scared to tell me?"

"Of course not!" she laughed, "you're perfect. I love you so much. We're perfect for each other. This isn't about us, it's about doing the right thing. Now, when should I book our appointment?"

"Are you serious?" she was dead serious, "you do realize this is the only thing we ever argued about?"

"Mm," she agreed and we wheeled the cart to checkout, "so let's practice resolving arguments."

It was a trap. There was no way out.

Sunday, one p.m. We sat across from a random woman—
"not random," Rivka scolded me afterward when we spoke
about the session, "she's got her doctorate from Columbia,
Dr. Diane Schwartz,"—in an office painted peach and cheery.

"I'm sure you're nervous," she looked from me to Rivka,
"or excited to begin. This session we're just going to get to
know each other a bit better."

So we discussed our relationship to this woman—about
how we understood each other's needs and went out of our
way to make sure the other was comfortable, and always
compromised by finding solutions that worked for both of
us, and pushed each other to do the right thing in a
respectful and understanding manner—and all the while, I
tried not to think about the hundred fifty dollars this cost us.

"Shall I pencil you in for next Sunday?"

"Perfect," Rivka said with a grin.

Or the many more hundred fifties we would spend.

The Other Woman

I wouldn't have thought anything of it. I would have glanced at it and moved on, except... except as much as I wanted to ignore it, I couldn't. This wasn't the first time something like this had happened.

I looked again at the name and phone number scribbled in Dovid's distinctive scrawl. Karen Lee. The area code suggested it was a local number. And the name? A *shiksa*. I wondered if that made me feel better or worse but mostly I felt an empty sort of helplessness. On a whim, I dialed the number. No—I panicked and ended the call before it even went through.

I couldn't do this. I couldn't pretend anymore. I paced back and forth in our five-foot kitchen.

Karen Lee. I could picture her in my head. Tall, long dark hair and long toned legs. Dovid was into legs. I could tell by the way he caressed mine. But I was short! And my ankles were wide and Dovid always said I was perfect but what if Karen was more perfect? What if she was exactly what he wanted—physically, I mean. Dovid could never otherwise be attracted to a *shiksa.*

I filled a big mug of steaming tea and collapsed onto one of our flimsy wooden chairs. Our kitchen set was a hand-me-down from Dovid's sister and creaked of old age whenever in use.

I would do it tonight. A proper confrontation. Except there was nothing proper about this. I almost choked. My husband, my beautiful husband of only one year. I chose a strong frum boy, one with *yiras shamayim* and more importantly, always *makpid* on *shmiras einayim.* He was an excellent learner and always helped around the house too. At nights he worked in a yeshiva to make some extra money. Always working so hard. Always focused on a goal—our goal. But recently these dirty secrets kept creeping up on our quality time. Like, can he at least *try* to be discreet?

"I'll be home at seven," he'd say on the phone and then bound through the door a half-hour past.

"Where were you?" I'd ask casually.

"Helping a neighbor," or, "got caught up talking to Baruch at *shul*," or, most infuriatingly, "oh, am I late?"

They came to him almost too easily—the excuses. Those off-handed responses that made my blood boil.

Karen Lee. What excuse would he have now?

I almost cried. But I was too shocked to cry. I was too angry. Instead I took a scalding gulp of tea. It was one thing to schmooze with another woman—as he did with Shira Shwatzbaum—another to write her number down in that intimate way. It made me imagine what other intimate things they shared. Dovid and this random woman he got off the streets! Oh, *Hashem*. I cried.

Shira Shwatzbaum was the babysitter. We used her to watch baby Rochelle, but only when we really needed to— just to go to family *simchas*. It was fine. She was sixteen and very mature, a family friend's daughter.

Oh, *Hashem*. I buried my hands in my face. She was *very* mature, I realized the night Dovid and I came back late from Zelig's bar mitzvah.

"Thank you so much, Shira," I said, "sorry we stayed out longer than planned."

"It's okay," she smiled. That's when I noticed, Shira really grew up. Her smile was stunning, her thick hair pulled back in a modest ponytail and her shirt buttoned till the top, but still, I could make out the shape of a very developed chest underneath.

"I'll drive you home," Dovid said after I paid her and I wished like I never wished before that I had a license so I could drive her home myself.

Shira lived just seven minutes away. So why did it take Dovid twenty-six to come back? Why? Each minute passed painstakingly slowly, each a deliberate blow to the safety net my mind created telling me everything was okay, Dovid wasn't that kind of guy, I had to *trust* him. Trust him when he told me he dropped off Shira and went to fill up gas. Ha!

Karen Lee.

Vashti was a beautiful *shiksa* too until then she got pimples and a tail and Achashverosh never wanted her again. How would Karen look with pimples and a tail? I smirked despite myself.

The clock ticked past ten. Dovid had a shift at the yeshiva tonight. He was due home the latest at ten-thirty—I hoped. Unless he found another reason to stay out late.

I busied myself by looking through the bills, calculating how we would get through the month. Didn't Dovid realize we had enough on our minds? Without his sneaking around?

Karen Lee. Did he just get the number or has it sat in his pocket for a while? The corners of the paper were yellowed. It didn't mean anything though, the paper itself could be old while the number fresh. And how had the exchange been? Had she leaned over to whisper it into his ear for him to take down? Did she flatter him, "you're so easy to speak to, we should definitely speak more"? Where could he have picked up such a woman, my pure, innocent-seeming Dovid?

How many times had they met up already? Or was it just that once when she gave him the number? I couldn't bear the thought of my husband with this strange woman. I hoped for our family's sake and for the sake of Dovid's *olam haba* that it was just one chat—still nauseating to imagine.

I examined the credit card bill thoroughly. Two weeks ago there was a charge for twenty dollars at a café. I didn't go to a café. I felt faint.

Did he call her sweetie like he called me?

Did he meet her on line in the supermarket?

He was out of yeshiva too much, helping out with domestic tasks too much. That was for a woman. The man needed to stay in yeshiva. It was safe there. Especially a man with a darling smile like Dovid. His front tooth jutted out in such a charming way. And his cheeks! How could any woman resist those sweet puffed cheeks?

Did he open the door for her when they went to that café to sit down for a cup of coffee? And whose idea was it? Hers or his?

It was hers, I knew it, she was a manipulative *shiksa*. He didn't understand what he was doing—but she was beautiful too! And he wanted her!

Oh, *Hashem*.

My tea got cold. I spilled it down the sink.

A few minutes later a key turned in the lock. Dovid stepped inside, a huge grin on his face.

"Hello to you, my beautiful wife!" he beamed.

I looked down at the bills and scribbled notes to look busy.

He hummed as he pulled the couscous from the fridge. With a plastic fork, he ate straight from the container. Once the couscous was gone, he washed the plastic container and let it dry on the rack. Only then he turned and really looked at me.

"How are you doing my sweetie?"

That's what did it. I snapped—I cried and cried and couldn't stop.

"What happened?" he kneeled on his knee beside me and looked up.

"You're—" I sniffled "—you're not supposed to kneel," I reminded him. It was a *goyish* custom. That made the tears fall faster.

He sat on a chair instead and reached for my hand, "won't you tell me what's wrong?"

I pulled my hand away like I did whenever he crassly grabbed for me. What's wrong? He was mocking me. He was forcing me to verbalize the horrible things he'd done. My eyes hurt. My head hurt.

"Please, can you speak to me?" he grasped his own hands tight.

I couldn't speak. I pushed the number forward on the table.

"Oh! Did she call? Is it ready?"

"What?"

"I gave our stuff in last week, remember? You're dress, my suit? You wanted to get them dry-cleaned," he continued when I didn't respond, "she said it would be ready next week but we could check in to see if it's ready earlier."

I swallowed, "she didn't call."

"Okay," he bit his lip, his front tooth sticking out in a way that made my heart stammer, "Did you need the dress for something? I could get it back."

"No," I said, "next week is fine."

"I don't understand," Dovid tried again, "can you tell me what's wrong?"

Finally, I said, "I don't let you learn enough, it's not right. You have to stay in yeshiva more. It's a *zechus* for both of us."

"I learn all day."

I shook my head, "you go to the supermarket, I send you to the cleaners, I send you to bring Rochelle to daycare—" I hiccupped, "I'll walk her with the carriage. You can't go there anymore."

Mrs. Rothstein, the head of the daycare, was a fine woman, still young at 34, with good hands and flashy *tichels*. Not a place for a man to frequent, especially a man as swayable as dear Dovid.

"I want to help you out," he said, "you work so hard."

I shut my eyes and tried to take his words at face value, and not for the horrid subtext that lay beneath—that he wanted to see Mrs. Rothstein again.

Karen Lee might not be the tall, gorgeous woman of Dovid's dreams (and my demise) but I was putting too many *nisyonos* in front of this eager-to-please man. Setting him up to schmooze with all these women, to do the sin most unimaginable.

"Just don't," I whispered, "Stop trying to help all the time. You're making things worse."

Fit For Each Other

Shaindy was different, I realized with a start. It's the kind of thing that creeps up on you slowly and then slaps you in the face. The slap came on a Thursday night. We'd gone out with two other couple friends, sitting on the deck of a restaurant, laughing, drinking and eating. I laughed along with everyone. Nach's wife wore a dress with little flowers on it and smiled like a queen. Ashy's wife, as always, wore high heels to add inches to her thin, tiny frame. And Shaindy...

I looked at Shaindy and grimaced. Her lipstick spread out of its lines, eyes tired, even as she laughed—even her shiny *sheitel* looked limp. But that was all surface-level stuff. I barely cared about any of those things. What I *did* care about was her body.

I sighed, thinking back to where it started. It happened after having Benny. I mean, already while she was pregnant I noticed her thighs growing disproportionately and the stretch marks on her side, but I kept my mouth shut. I knew these things happened to women. But after having the baby, it's like Shaindy gave up. Her stomach was still big and round, her arms all doughy and soft. The few dresses that fit her stretched awkwardly across her grown hips.

"Do you want some?" Shaindy pushed her desert towards me. It was a chocolate waffle and at once I felt sick. I quickly accepted it so I wouldn't have to see her eat it and watch the sugary sauce dripping down her chin.

Like a termite, once the thought got into my head, I couldn't get it out, it just consumed my whole mind. That week I thought of little else. As she left for the store still dressed in her maternity clothes, as she sat with the baby like a lump on the couch, as she crawled into bed with one of my t-shirts, filling it a little *too* nicely.

And thus, I began to dread the impending *mikvah* night.

153

How could I touch her like this? How could I admit that I was suddenly *not* attracted to my wife? Suddenly repelled by her? I didn't understand how Shaindy could let herself go, but more than anything, I blamed myself for not seeing the beauty in her the way her body changed. I hated myself for it.

But I always knew bigger women were not for me! That's why I was relieved when I found Shaindy, a skinny girl, and better yet, she had *always* been thin! I saw back in pictures from high school and seminary. While all the other girls grew large overly sugared pastries and potato burekas, my Shaindy remained thin. How could I have guessed that one baby was all it would take to literally tip the scale?

"Shaindy," I said gently, the night before *mikvah*. It was better to get it over with beforehand and not be put on the spot. She was in bed, watching a show from the laptop resting on her large thighs. "Remember that diet you were on?"

She looked up sharply, "was I?"

"Um…" I racked my brain, "something with milk."

"You mean how I'm lactose intolerant?"

"Oh yeah, so how is it going for you now?"

"I take lactates," she said, pausing the voices from her laptop, "you see me take them whenever we go for pizza. You didn't realize?" she raised a brow.

Now that she mentioned it, I do vaguely remember her popping pills around dairy. But how do I bring up dieting now? My upper lip started sweating as I scrambled for an idea, apologizing profusely as I did, "I'm sorry, I didn't mean... I don't know why I brought it up. Diet? What diet? You never diet!"

In the end, I didn't have to.

Shaindy cut me off: "You think I'm fat." It was less of a question, more of a statement. Her thick arms drooped at her sides.

"Hey," I held my hands up to defend myself from her dagger eyes, "you said it!"

"Well, what do you want from me?" she demanded. The laptop wobbled dangerously on her legs, "I gave birth two months ago!"

"Well," I bit my lip, "how long are you planning... on staying like this?" I gestured to her body.

She cursed and cursed again. I colored. Shaindy only curses when she stubs her toe real bad or burns something she's cooking.

"You," she said, gaining volume as she spoke, "gained fifty pounds since we got married. What's your excuse?"

"Hey!" I protested, "That's not fair. I'm a *man*," I stressed the word, "I don't have to be all pretty and dressed up like you. It doesn't bother anyone."

"Well, you know what?" she stood up, "it bothers *me*, fatty! Go on a diet and tell me how it feels, or better yet, go on a diet while you're *freaking* nursing our baby and everyone is shoving food down your throat so you have energy to *move*."

I flinched.

"Go on!" she continued, "don't eat the whole pan of potato *kugel* on Shabbos. You've already eaten enough for the year." She paused to breathe, "I'm happy you brought this up because I would never have had the nerve otherwise. I've gained fifteen pounds since the day we got married and I'll lose it like that," she snapped her fingers, "but you," she stabbed a finger at me, "you'll remain a fatty until you have a heart attack at the age of forty unless you go back to the gym first. And the nerve of you, oh G-d."

"You're right," I hung my head, "I will diet... if you do," I added hopefully.

She rolled her eyes and pressed play on her show, "sure."

I could barely hold back my grin. Potato *kugel*? So I wouldn't let Shaindy see me eat it! I'd be careful around her and snack around my friends. And Shaindy, she always stuck to her word. She'd shed those pounds in no time. I sighed, relieved.

Shared Value

"Look what I found for Malky's wedding," I pulled the gown out of its bag and twirled it around. My best friend Malky just got engaged—*baruch Hashem*—and I was going to be a bridesmaid! She told me the color right away so I could start looking for a dress.

"How much was it?" Shaya asked, barely glancing in my direction. He was lying on his bed, deeply engrossed in a biography of the Chofetz Chaim.

"It actually wasn't so much… in comparison. You wouldn't believe the prices of these things! I shopped with Leah and Zahava and each of their gowns cost triple mine."

I looked at my gown, it reached the floor in shimmering tulle, purple like all of the bridesmaids. Looking at it now, out of the shops with hundreds of options, it did look a little less fancy than I'd have liked. The fabric was synthetic, the seams were messy. Leah's dress had a full sequin top. Zahava's was an expensive lace.

"How much was it?" he asked again.

"Well," I fumbled with the tag, "it was supposed to be six hundred! Can you believe it? But it was on sale for four-fifty. And then I asked for a discount! So she gave me an additional fifteen percent off," I said proudly.

"You spent three hundred eighty shekels on that thing?" finally he looked up, examining the fabric so intently, I cringed. The lilac purple that so caught my eye suddenly looked faded and worn in this lighting.

"It looks really good on," I assured.

"I'm sure it does," Shaya said slowly, "but that's not the problem." He closed his *sefer* and put it aside, "the problem is that I told you that you can spend two hundred shekels on a dress. You spent a hundred eighty more."

"Two hundred shekel could barely buy a Shabbos dress! This is for a *wedding*."

"And you never went to a wedding before? You don't have *any* dresses you could possibly wear?"

"I'm a bridesmaid!" I hung the dress carefully and stuck it in the closet, out of sight, "I need the color."

"No," Shaya said, "what you *need* to do is return this dress and find something for two hundred shekels. So buy a grey Shabbos dress. I'm sure nobody will mind."

"Grey? What grey? This is *purple*," I groaned, "You just don't get these things because you're a man."

"And you don't get money because you're a woman!" Shaya shot back, "now put that dress back in the bag. You're taking it back tomorrow."

His voice rang with finality, his mouth a thin line. There was no arguing with Shaya when he was like this. He sat up and waited until the dress was carefully folded and back in its bag, only then did he go back to his *sefer*.

I went to the bathroom, locked the door, put the cover over the toilet and sat there, waiting for my storm of indignant emotions to pass. Yes, it would be terribly embarrassing to wear a simple dress to the wedding, even more so because Leah and Zahava knew I'd bought this one. They would wonder why I'd switched. I would never be able to tell them the reason. But this was my husband and I had to respect his wishes. Why did he sometimes have to make them so hard to respect?

The next day, after hours of re-teaching an elderly woman to write and filling out mounds of paperwork, I drove forty-five minutes opposite the direction of home. It took another ten minutes to find parking and another fifteen to locate the specific store I got the gown from on the street of gown shops that all looked the same.

It took another two minutes for the old stern lady to tell me that there were no refunds, she pointed to the big sign behind her that reinforced her point. No refund. All sales are final.

On the drive home I felt both triumphed and ashamed... but mainly ashamed.

Shaya was in a good mood that evening. I didn't break the atmosphere by telling him about the dress just yet. He had prepared mashed potatoes in my absence and offered me a bowl.

"Have a seat, relax! You work too hard," he said, "If they keep you this late again, I'm *not* going to let you go back to that work," he laughed.

I didn't laugh. This was my first job after three years of schooling and I had no intention of leaving.

"I didn't finish now, I actually finished earlier..." I said. But now he would ask where I'd been and I'd have to begrudgingly bring up the dress again. I braced myself—

But Shaya didn't ask, in fact, he whistled as he scooped himself another bowl of mashed potatoes. Something happened, I knew it, and Shaya was just waiting for me to prompt him so he could burst with the news.

"You had a good day?" I asked with a slight smile.

"Oh, the best," Shaya grinned, "I put up a pergola for that Rabbi Grossman, what a wonderful family. And the Rabbi was telling me that he and his wife go away once a year, even after thirty-two years. Isn't that nice? And I thought, how long are we married for? Less than a year. But did we ever go away? We're just both always working so hard. Working, working, working. And you know what? We deserve a reward! Don't we? So I booked a little getaway. A *tzimmer* in the north, just for the weekend," his smile grew as he spoke and in the end, he was beaming.

It was hard not to beam back, even though a *tzimmer* up north in December wasn't my ideal vacation, so I said with all the enthusiasm I could muster, "wow, that's so exciting! When are we going?"

"This weekend."

"We're supposed to eat a meal by Bubby."

"So explain to her the situation, she'll understand."

"What if she doesn't?" I pressed.

"I'll talk to her. She can't get upset at her brand new grandson-in-law."

"Okay then..." and then I asked casually, "How much did it cost?"

"It's nothing for you to worry about," Shaya waved his hand, "we deserve this."

I didn't bring up the dress that night.

"Before you go," Shaya called, "I'm going to give you an extra fifty shekels for this week's shopping, okay?" he fished for his wallet and pulled out a crisp bill. We didn't discuss the dress again but he saw it hanging in the closet and ever since was trepidatious about leaving me with the card. Instead he gave me cash. A hundred to fill the car with gas, twenty to buy something for lunch, ten to get some milk on the way home and twenty to always have on me as emergency money.

"We'll need something special for our trip. Extra snacks, but not those apple chips you always buy."

"I buy them because I *like* them."

"They're overpriced and taste like paper. Get something we both like."

Every Thursday night, while Shaya went to a *shiur*, I did the shopping. It was annoying to go alone but I preferred that Shaya learned. Besides, it wasn't too difficult. Shaya did all the homework beforehand. He wrote out the budget and a specific shopping list. I tried sneaking things here and there—a container of olives, or some juicy grapes, or, of course, apple chips, my favorite, but nothing went by Shaya unnoticed.

If the budget was stretched by twenty shekels, I'd have to go back to return something. At the beginning of our marriage I was shocked, even outraged:

"I am not going back to return a tray of eggs!" I'd fold my arms and sulk in the kitchen like a little girl.

"I wrote that we need twelve eggs," Shaya would stab the list with his finger, "you bought thirty."

"So what if I did?" In my house, we always say it's better to have too much than too little. My mother always over-shopped, lugging so many kilos of vegetables and fruits from the supermarket, we barely had a chance to finish them by the time they'd start to rot.

Shaya had a different upbringing, "first of all, in *my* house, we don't just waste. We don't buy a million things and wait for them to go bad. That's *bal tashchis.* But it's not just about the eggs. I gave you a certain amount of money to spend. You spend too much. How am I supposed to do my job of supporting you if you don't listen to the guidelines I make?"

"Hate to break it to you," I laughed, "but this is the twenty-first century and we're both working to support *each other.*"

"But we're *frum*," Shaya would stress the word as if explaining it to a child, "We don't do whatever everyone in the twenty-first century does. We have a Torah and the Torah has specific guidelines. And one of the things it says is that the man owns the money. Everything you make, everything I make, *I* have to take care of. So when you go out spending all that money without my permission, how do you expect that makes me feel?"

I'd shrug.

"It makes me feel like I'm not doing my job right. Like I'm not being a good husband. So please, just trust me. A man has to support his wife with everything that she needs. I take care of the money because I take care of you."

True to his word, Shaya usually gave me enough money to get what I needed. *Usually.* I thought sourly of the purple gown in our closet.

I drove to the supermarket and started picking things off the list:

Jarred gefilte fish, the kind Shaya eats.

Peppers, cucumbers. Never tomatoes. Those made Shaya sick.

Apples. The rest of the fruit was too expensive. I examined the shelves hoping to find another fruit on sale. The tangerines were cheap. But then I thought against it. If Shaya and I were going to spend the whole weekend together, I'd better get exactly what he wanted so he wouldn't sulk.

Maybe this is what marriage was about? The compromises we make for each other. We both had different upbringings and backgrounds, so of course, it was hard to understand sometimes but Shaya really did his best to do his job right in this marriage. I respected that, even as I passed by the apple chips longingly. Instead, I chose Shaya's favorite *Bisly*. That would put him in a good mood.

Novel Idea

I wrinkled my nose as I stepped inside the house. The neighbors were blasting their *goyish* pop music. I heard it all the way in our living room.

"Elana," I called, "I'm home." As if they read my angry thoughts, finally those neighbors shut the horrid song.

"Hey," Elana smiled, coming to greet me with baby Mosh in her arms.

I kissed his cheek, "my little *tzadik*," and smiled at Elana, "my *aishes chayil*."

It was good to be home after a long day. We sat around the kitchen table and ate the delicious mushroom barley soup that Elana prepared.

"How is work going?" I asked kindly. Not in a way that would pressure her, I knew how easily pressured she was—when she worked too much and when she worked too little. I just wanted to know how her day went.

She grimaced, "it's slow, I'm not getting any jobs recently. I don't know why." She bit her lip, forehead creased. Elana was a freelance writer and usually had a steady stream of work, but not this month. A major client backed out. Another said they'd reach out to her in two months when they were more 'ready' to proceed. Elana's face brightened—"I started writing a novel though!"

"Why, that's amazing! What about?" my wife, a novelist? Our Rabbi's wife, Gitty, wrote books too. They were beautifully illustrated children's books about the creation of the world, about Avraham and Sara, Yitchak and Rivka. The whole community had at least one copy of them in their homes. Elana was so talented, she could do something like that too.

Elana laughed and turned pink, "oh nothing, it's just for me, for fun. I'm not planning on publishing it anyway."

"Tell me!" I protested.

"It's an action romance novel," she laughed again, "hmm, how can I explain the plot? It's about Evan Parker and Sherry Woods. They live in the Midwest. She works at a diner off the highway and he always stops by for a coffee and a chat. But then she notices he carries a gun and his fingernails are always dirty. So she follows him one time and... Well, I didn't get so far but that's the start."

I looked down and raised my eyebrows, "well. That sounds quite..." I didn't finish my sentence. I didn't know how to.

"Quite what?" she pressed.

"What made you think of such a story? Evan Parker? Sherry Woods? Sweetie, tell me, what in the world made you think of such things?"

She shrugged, "I like those kinds of books. I thought it would be interesting... to write one myself. Y'know, just to see how it goes."

"Elana, even if you don't publish the book, even if you just write it for *yourself*..." I pursed my lips, "these things have an effect on your *neshama*. Everything you write, you're writing it on your soul. What's the point of thinking and writing about Sherry Schmuck when you could write about *our* people? *Our* history... *Yiddishe* things."

Elana looked everywhere but me, like a student found guilty in the principal's office. Well, better guilty before me than guilty before The Almighty.

"Let's just forget it for now," she said after a minute, "Tell me about your day."

"Work was fine," I waved a hand dismissively, I worked as a travel agent and work was always the same, "let me tell you what I learned in my *shiur* this morning. A fascinating story about the *parsha*."

And I was off, mending the broken air at the table. Broken with talks of a *shtus* novel. I spoke in length about *our* people in the desert, wanderers, sinners. Korach and his sons.

"Ah," Elana said, and sometimes, "mmm."

I knew what she was doing and it made my heart ache. She was fake listening.

I retired to bed early and lay there twisting and turning, wondering, where did I go wrong?

Elana and I weren't exactly the same but we always had the same values. She came from a family where the men wore colored shirts, where the boy cousins and the girl cousins played board games together on Shabbos, where the kids watched cable TV. I knew all of this before we even started dating, but the *shadchan* assured me that Elana was different from her family. And at the start, I believed it too. She always said *Asher Yatzar* after the bathroom. From our very first date, I'd observed her lips mouthing the blessing to herself. She *bench*ed from a *bencher*. She wore long sleeves and even longer skirts. These, I concluded, were signs that Elana was right for me.

But how could I expect, when we finally got married and moved in together, that she would want Wifi in our home? *It's for work*, she told me. *Work*. I scoffed, checking the browsing history to my growing despair—Facebook. Reddit. Youtube! I closed the laptop and shut my eyes. What would bring a good wife to behave like this? Maybe it was Hashem's way of punishing me? No—maybe I wasn't giving her enough attention! That must have been it.

So it was decided, I needed to pay my wife the utmost attention.

I woke up at two a.m. Bleary-eyed and confused. Mosh had been crying. Now he was silent. I peeked over at Elana and gasped.

"What?" she whispered, also half asleep.

"What's wrong with you?" I looked away from her, completely exposed as she was nursing, "cover up! Have some modesty." I couldn't see my wife like this during *niddah*.

"Oh shut up," she grumbled.

I rolled over, my mind reeling from what I saw. The situation was worse than I thought.

For the next week, I observed. I didn't speak much. I couldn't speak. It was like the dam broke in my head—once I noticed one thing, the rest was glaringly clear. Had there been any signs beforehand? Did my parents predict this would happen? And if yes, why didn't they say anything? Why didn't they warn me?

Why did all these dirty desires come out two years too late?

I cooked with Elana on Friday as part of my *Giving Her Attention* plan. She put me to work cutting onions. I was so concentrated, I barely noticed when she did it—she tossed the dill into the chicken soup.

"Was that washed?" I cried.

"Of course."

"With soap? And soaked in water for ten minutes?"

"I make soup every week and you eat it," she said, "so stop doubting me now. I know how to wash dill."

I looked at the soup, dill floating on top. With minuscule bugs in the water? I felt sick. That night I didn't touch the soup. Nor did I touch the salmon Elana made, nor her olive dip. I stuck to chummus on challa, both with a *hechsher* I could rely on.

In less than a week my home felt like a foreign land with food I couldn't trust.

Now Mosh was too young to eat this food. But what would be when he started eating solids? His mother would feed him the food she cooked with all her leniencies? Across the table, Elana started nursing Mosh—under a proper cloth, thank goodness—and I realized with a start, I was too late. Mosh ate what Elana ate, all from the same source—*treif* dill.

I had to give Elana more attention. I focused on my goal. It was the only thing that could fix this—this thing that seemed irreparably broken.

"I want to help you clean," I told Elana one night.

"I clean the house before you get home."

"So wait for me one night," I smiled, "we can do it together."

"No problem!"

And so we did. The following evening, Elana supplied me with a rag and spray and she took out the bucket with water.

"You do this every day?" I said. No wonder she felt resentful.

Elana laughed, "no, but if you're helping, we might as well do a deep cleaning."

She instructed me where to spray, how to properly scrub the countertops, how to clean the sinks.

And then she got her phone to play music. I froze.

"Oh, does this bother you?" she switched the song to something Hebrew. But it was too late, I already heard enough of the first song. It was a dreaded pop song, much like the one I heard just days ago. The one that the 'neighbors' played.

"Elana," she didn't turn, humming to the Hebrew song, sweeping the floors, "Elana!"

"What's wrong? Yalla, get to work!"

"That song that you played before. Do you always listen to that around here?"

174

"What?" she squinted her eyes at me.

"That first one you put on…"

"Oh! You mean that old Taylor Swift?" she laughed, "I love it *so* much more than her new stuff. It's like the soundtrack of my high school years."

"You play that around here?" I couldn't keep my voice level, "you play that *around Mosh??*"

She put a hand on my shoulder. I threw it off, "don't touch me, you *shiksa* girl. First, you've corrupted our son, now you're going to try and corrupt me?"

"What are you even saying?" Elana rolled her eyes, "can you calm down and clean? It was your idea to help in the first place."

"Elana! You will not ignore me like that. I'm asking how you can play such music around *our* son. Our little *tzadik*?" Did this woman care at all?

"What do you want from me! I'm with him all day, so yeah, he sees a bit of Youtube, he hears some Taylor Swift," she smirked and added, "he even helps me brainstorm for my book!"

"This isn't a joke."

"Who's laughing?"

I looked down, at my shoes, at her skirt. Even those long skirts that once consoled me grew shorter by the day. So I told her, "your skirts are getting shorter—"

"Thanks for noticing," she hissed, "this is the same skirt I've been wearing since we got married. I gained some weight—now all the men on the street can get a better glimpse at my fat calves. Oh no!"

"What happened to us?" I whispered, "what happened to our goals? To the home we wanted to build? Why are you so willing to just turn away from it all?"

"Why are you so dramatic?" she shot back, "every little thing is a huge deal to you. I'm sorry I'm not a perfect mother. I'm sorry I'm not a perfect person."

"You think I care about that? Nothing matters to me as long as I see you're at least *trying*! That's all Hashem cares about! But you're not trying. You're doing nothing. Worse than nothing! You're bringing us down. The whole family. You're influencing Mosh will all these *goyishe* things, you're influencing yourself. You're drawing yourself away from me, into your own little world. Well," I turned away, "I hope you like it there."

It was our biggest fight to date. I'd assumed once I'd confronted her, it would sort itself out. It didn't. We didn't talk for the next three days, just passed each other in complete silence. We ate dinner at different times. She played music sometimes at night, just to rub it in. She held the baby, she played with him. She showed him something on her computer screen. I was reeling. I was fuming. I did nothing.

"You want him?" she said, "so take him. You watch him."

She stood up and came towards me. I folded my arms and looked away. "Put him down," I demanded but she came closer and I yelled desperately, "you know I can't take him, just put him down!"

And she did, she dumped him on me.

I held Mosh wriggling in my arms, aghast at my wife. Had she gone so far as to disregard *niddah*? She knew we couldn't pass things from hand to hand, even our child. But that was the problem, wasn't it? Elana knew a lot and did a little.

"My little *tzadik*, my little *tzadik*," I cooed in Mosh's ear as Elana took her laptop to the living room. *Not for long*, a voice whispered in my own ear, *not with a mother like that*.

Three days. And then it was Shabbos again.

I made the final decision after a trip to the bathroom. On Friday, there was toilet paper on the roll and now the roll was empty. Since sundown, I, of course, had only used tissues. Who used the toilet paper? Who ripped the toilet paper on our precious Shabbos?

It couldn't be anyone else but my once *frum* wife.

Kosher, *Taharas Hamishpachah* and now Shabbos too? These were the foundations of a Jewish home. If you let them go, you let it all go. Soon her hair would be uncovered and her skirt above her knees, I just knew it. Already wisps of hair escaped her snood.

I had to make an urgent call once Shabbos was over—not that I was planning for after Shabbos, nor anticipating Shabbos to end, *chas v'shalom*. But, I had an urgent call to make to the *Beis Din*.

Anonymous Post

Looking for recommendations for a *frum* sex therapist.

Some background information: my husband and I got married three years ago and ever since sex has been a sore topic between us—literally. It took us weeks of trying to actually do it the first time because each time I'd freak out and all my muscles would seize up down there. When we finally managed I felt like I was being torn through.

I try to relax and say it's okay but every time we try, it hurts me so bad, and sometimes we just can't do it at all. He feels so guilty for hurting me but also upset. I also feel guilty all the time, knowing I can't give him what he needs. I try as hard as I could to pretend it doesn't hurt but sometimes I can't hide it and we have to stop.

He used to say, "Its fine," but now he doesn't even say that anymore. Now he just turns his head away. "Don't look away from me," I want to tell him, "I don't want to do this to you!" but I know ultimately it's all my fault. He could've had an amazing sex life with any other woman.

The last time we tried, I cried and stopped him. We couldn't speak for days afterwards. That was months ago. I don't know what's wrong with me, why Hashem made me like this. I feel so broken and don't know if I can ever be fixed.

I thought it would get better over time, I thought it might fade but it's not.

We never speak about it with anyone because it is just too embarrassing, but it's so hard battling this alone and it's not getting better. It is the biggest strain on our marriage and I'm afraid if we don't get help soon, our marriage will just fall apart.

Please post contact info if you know anyone that can help us and I will reach out. TIA!

Inconceivable Notions

We waited in the uncomfortable chairs for the couple before us to finish at the desk. It had been twenty minutes already. They were taking their sweet time.

"This is ridiculous, they can't keep us waiting forever!" Pessy groaned, "You know what I think? I think the bank does this on purpose to get people to give up—they make you wait so long so you give up and go home! It's like that with everything, isn't it? Banks... kids."

There it was. She'd brought it up. Kids. And I was suddenly tired.

"What? You don't think so?" she challenged, "you don't think Hashem makes things *deliberately* difficult so that people give up?"

"Of course He could test you..." I said, choosing my words carefully, "but only because He knows you can overcome whatever He puts before you. I don't think *anyone* should ever give up." *And that's why we won't give up trying for kids,* I thought but didn't add.

"Hmm... but imagine we waited in these chairs for years, just waiting to speak to that guy behind the desk. At what point should we stand up and say, 'forget it, Hashem clearly doesn't want us to get this mortgage'?"

I was saved from answering. The couple at the desk got up and it was our turn to take their place.

Dan—as his nametag read—was very helpful. He explained the whole process to us, what we should expect and how to avoid problems.

"Now sign these and we can finalize everything," he pushed forward some forms, "this one is to confirm your income, just for the bank to make sure you make enough to pay us back—"

"Yes, we could afford this damn house, what other expenses do we have?" Pessy snapped. I shot her a look.

"Of course," Dan said, "this is just protocol." He pushed forward the rest of the forms for us to sign—"initials here, date here, full name here."

We signed everything. Dan said he'd let us know when the forms go through and if they need anything else. He smiled as he concluded, "And then I'll have to congratulate you two on becoming homeowners."

"Why are we even buying a house if we have no kids to fill it with?" Pessy muttered as we headed out.

"Maybe have some hope and things will work out."

"So now you're blaming me?" Pessy raised her voice. A woman on line at the teller turned in alarm.

"I never said that! Stop it. This is *not* the place."

"It's never the place," Pessy whimpered.

"I'm sorry," Pessy said as she got into the passenger's seat, fumbling with her hands, her skirt, her purse. Anything to avoid her eyes from tearing—but there it was, her eyes welled up.

I sat behind the steering wheel, frozen solid for a minute. Sometimes I was jealous of my wife—at the ease in which she cried and expressed her emotions. I felt everything, it overwhelmed me, and then I felt nothing.

"I know," I said eventually, "me too."

Pessy and I were married for nearly two and a half years. We had no kids.

For the first year that was great. Pessy wanted to wait anyways. I was a bit wary at first, not wanting to deter any *mitzvah*, especially one as explicitly clear in the Torah as '*pru urvu, be fruitful and multiply,*' but Pessy assured me, "my *kallah* teacher said it's a totally normal thing to wait. Because there are so many divorces nowadays—not that we'll get divorced! *Chas v'shalom*! But couples should spend the first year getting to know each other better before they have kids."

A year passed. We spent it with weekends away and romantic date nights. Evenings with friends and long, lazy Shabbos afternoons. It was a beautiful time. And so, convinced we knew each other as well as we possibly could, we were ready for a child.

A child never came.

We waited for months.

"It will happen this month," Pessy would say and read through the *Tehillim*.

"This is the month," she'd say the following month, "did you finish your *Tehillim* for today?"

"I have a feeling about this month," she'd come home from the *mikveh*, glowing and excited. I was determined not to disappoint. *This* month. The month came and passed.

"I think it's normal," I tried to reassure her, "these things don't always happen right away."

"I know," she sighed, "I just always thought it would be easy. All those sixteen-year-olds on reality shows do it by accident. Why can't we do it if we're *trying*?"

I looked heavenward and directed the question to Him.

Until one day Pessy took out her calendar and brandished it to me as if it was some sort of evidence.

"What's this?"

"It's finished!" she cried, "a year passed. A full year!"

"Okay," I said slowly.

"No, not okay," Pessy shot back, "we tried a year and *nothing*. Do you know what this means? We have a problem. Something is wrong with me... or you. Or us. We need to get checked out."

"Okay," I said again, "we'll get checked out. We'll take care of this."

There was something relieving about it. We'd get checked out. A doctor would tell us our problem and offer a solution.

Whether it was hard or easy, at least we'd know what we had to do.

That was four months ago.

The specialist sat us down and asked us a few questions. She was a *frum* doctor and had a reputable record with many couples. They were easy questions, about our history, about Pessy's cycle.

"I just don't want to take any hormones," Pessy burst, "I was on birth control for a few months right when we got married and it was *horrible*. I was so crazy and moody all the time. I felt like I didn't have control over myself. And I had crazy breakouts. Remember," she turned to me, "remember my crazy acne?"

"I try not to." Just as I tried not to remember crazy Pessy on birth control. She'd burst into tears at the most unexpected times. Like, everything would be fine. She'd open the fridge, discover that we were out of cheese, and start sniffling. And there was angry Pessy too—"*Why did you leave the bread bag opened? You know it dries out the bread!*" Her doctor offered her another brand but she gave up entirely. She consulted with her doctor, I consulted with my rabbi and we used spermicide instead.

"It seems you are both perfectly healthy," the specialist said, "look here," she told Pessy, "you have a twenty-three-day cycle. Shorter than the average but still perfectly normal. The problem is, you ovulate at around day ten."

I looked at Pessy to interpret. She looked just as blank as me.

The specialist rephrased, "your most fertile days are day seven to ten after menstruation."

"That can't be," Pessy said, "I'm still unclean by then."

"Yes," she nodded, "it can be. Many couples come to me with this problem. Don't worry, we find solutions for all of them.

Pessy nodded, "so what can we do?"

"First, you should go to your rabbi and speak to him about getting a *heter*—"

"I'm sorry, we're not those kinds of people," I interjected. Hashem created *taharas hamishpacha* to serve the family, not refuse us of a family.

"Excuse me, Mr. Steinman," she looked down at her papers to read the name right, "it is perfectly acceptable to get a *heter* to count four days instead of five—given Pessy has stopped bleeding—for the sake of conceiving. She will be able to go to the *mikveh* a day early. Eighty percent of the time, this helps. Speak to your rabbi about it. It's a pity to start treatment for an avoidable problem."

"We'll think about it," I said getting up.

But in the car ride home, it was clear. There was nothing to think about. I called our rabbi that evening.

"If it's really a problem..." he started when I asked.

"We've been trying for a year."

We received a *heter*.

More *tehillim*.

More trying.

More waiting.

I thought the hardest part of being unable to conceive was that there was no one to blame. It's not my fault. It's not her fault. It's just biology waiting for the optimal conditions.

But now I knew it wasn't biology that was holding us back. It was very hard not to freeze up during *shmoneh esrei* and cry out, "why, Hashem? Why do you do this to us? Why do we deserve this?"

I had to be strong, if not for me than for Pessy. As hard as I was taking it, she was taking it all the more hard.

Just last week she came back from an evening out with her friends, sobbing.

I hugged her tight and drew her to the couch. We'd had much more time than we'd planned on getting to know each other. If I knew one thing at this point, it was how to comfort my wife.

"What happened, dear?" I said eventually.

"They're all snobs—every last one of them!"

"Did they say something again?"

She sniffled and said through her tears, "It's like they all b-blame me! They think I ch-chose it, they think I don't want kids. We were talking about recipes and Baila told me, '*you* must have good recipes, you have all the time in the world.' And Ester said, 'I don't have a second to myself on Fridays,' then she looked straight at me and said, 'you'll understand when you have kids.'" Pessy heaved, "Why is everyone so m-mean?"

"Shhh," I rubbed circles on her back, "they didn't mean it. They don't know what we're going through, I'm sure if they did, they wouldn't act like that."

But even heard second-hand, Ester's words tore through my heart.

And it wasn't just her friends. She heard it from *her* mother, and my mother too. The disappointed looks at every

Shabbos table when Pessy sipped from the wine. I got a share of it too, but even then, they assumed it was just Pessy.

"You married a modern girl, didn't you," my mother said on the phone, "but just because she has a job doesn't mean she can't have kids. I had Mendy and Rochel while I was working full time, tell her that."

"I know Mom," I cringed, "we're talking about it."

"Are you?" she gushed, "I'll be the first to know, won't I?"

I was usually good at comforting Pessy—we were a team, getting through this together—but there were times when I was worse at it:

"Can you just go away?" she'd locked herself in the bathroom after getting her period. But an hour passed and I was concerned.

"Let's talk, please," I called through the door.

"Just leave me alone. I don't want to talk to anyone."

At those times it seemed the only person who could bring us comfort was one that wasn't born. I left her alone and suddenly felt lonely in our home of two.

"We could start you on treatment," the doctor said at our next visit, "don't worry, we have a really common drug. It's normally used in fertility treatment to induce ovulation, but it is helpful in this case because it has the side effect of delaying ovulation…" She explained a few options. This drug and that, and side effects and what couples usually decide on.

Finally, when she finished, Pessy folded her arms and said, "I'm not taking medicine. I am completely healthy. What else can we do?"

"That's not my domain," the specialist looked down at her papers, "I recommend you speak to a more lenient rabbi perhaps? Although it is hard to find rabbis lenient on such matters."

We stared at her for a moment, silent. Finally, I coughed and said, "Can you excuse us, we'll be right back."

"What do you mean, you're not taking medicine?" my whisper was heated, "We're at a doctor who can help us, who can prescribe something. What other choice do we have?"

"I want to see you take something!" she cried, "something that messes with your hormones and messes with your head."

"It won't do that. It will fix this," I said firmly, "Pessy, we'll finally have a baby!"

"How do you know?" she snapped, "Just go to the rabbi. Get us a *heter*."

"You know he won't allow waiting less than four days…"

The doctor printed us a prescription and we scheduled our next appointment. I took the prescription before Pessy could crumble it up.

"Oh," Pessy announced over dinner a week later, "my period came early."

"Yeah?" I took a bite of my schnitzel, "it never comes early."

"It did this month," she grinned.

"Are you… sure?" I looked into her eyes, holding her gaze carefully.

"What are you trying to say?"

"Nothing," I put my hands up, "I'm just wondering. You know how important this *mitzvah* is. It's the root of every Jewish home."

"Yes, and it's my body and my *mitzvah* so please stay out of it."

Four days and another seven she came home fresh from the *mikveh* glowing.

It was her *mitzvah*. I didn't say anything about the niggling doubt in my heart.

It was her *mitzvah*. I had to trust my wife.

Take My Breath Away

I was a *very* lucky woman. I have heard of all the horror stories—the men that shower just twice a week, or even *once*! The men with long toenails, the ones with smelly armpits and the ones with oily hair. The ones with back pimples and the ones with smelly feet. Bad farts and upset stomachs.

Getting married, you really don't know what you're getting into. These men show up on the date with a clean suit and a fresh haircut. You spend those few hours with them at different cafés. How could you tell that underneath their shirt is a forest of chest hair—the spikey dark curly type? How would you know that the moment their shoes come off, the house reeks of mold? The only thing you can do is walk down the aisle and hope for the best. During the seven circles around your *chosson*, you *daven* to Hashem with all your might that you've lucked out. That you've caught one of the clean ones.

I've heard all of the horror stories, but nope, I knew nothing of it. My husband, Asher was sparsely haired and squeaky clean. Hygiene was his *thing*. He showered daily, cleansed his skin, cut his toenails, and *always* brushed his teeth.

He'd jump up from bed and exclaim, "Let's go brush our teeth!"

"I already brushed," I was so lazy, already tucked in, my eyelids drooping.

"When?"

We both went to sleep early—another thing I'd lucked out with. We had the same sleep schedule! Never awake past eleven. I'd already been under my blanket by ten, "Dunno, an hour ago?"

"I like it when you come with me."

We'd brush our teeth together, our nightly routine, his figure behind my short frame, dwarfing it in the reflection. Both of us brushing back and forth thoroughly.

"I don't know what to do about it," Leora cried over the phone. It was the evening and I was speaking to my high school friend as I tidied up. Leora lived one of those horror stories and complained about it constantly. Her husband, Mordechai's, shoes stunk.

"Not just that," she ranted, "his feet smell horrible too! And then he lays on the bed with his smelly feet and I can't even breathe! It makes the whole room smell so bad. So I open the window, and guess what?" she continued without waiting for an answer, "He tells me he's cold! Well, I say that I've had it with him and his feet. You know what bothers me most? He doesn't even notice they reek!"

I cringed, "you really need to check out those feet sprays. They for sure have at the pharmacy."

"I've tried them all," she said brokenly.

We said goodbye and while I folded the few shirts left on our armchair, mourning for poor Leora's smelly fortune, Asher entered the room in all his showered glory, already clad in freshly laundered boxers and t-shirt. He brought in a whiff of Axe body wash with him.

Axe, aftershave, cologne. He wore it all in good taste. Never overdone, but always had me leaning in to inhale the deep musk.

"Want a mint strip?" he offered as he pulled one out for himself.

"Nah, they burn my tongue," I waved my hand dismissively.

"Try one," he insisted.

I carefully extracted one thin paper and stuck it in my mouth. It immediately stuck to the roof of my mouth and I scrambled for water.

"Ahhh." Relief as I downed my bottle.

"No! That's not how it works. You ruined it!" he was sucking his own coolly, folding his arms at me.

"Whatever," I shrugged and changed into pajamas myself.

Asher and I were married for nearly half a year now. We got over the awkward beginnings and fell into a more comfortable routine—coming home from work, talking over dinner, and relaxing at night.

Well, we mostly got over the awkward stuff. I glanced at Asher in the dark on the opposite end of the bed. He was turned away, said goodnight and remained silent.

Sometimes he got like this—distant. And not so in the mood of being intimate.

I worried. I fretted. I freaked out. I panicked. I particularly *was* in the mood that night. Very in the mood. It took fifteen minutes for me to outright say it:

"Do you wanna... kiss and stuff?" I asked, from my corner of the bed, trying not to sound too awkwardly hopeful.

Asher sighed.

"Is everything all right?"

"Yeah," he leaned over and kissed me for a moment. I closed my eyes—but he already pulled apart, "No."

"What's wrong?"

"I—" he stammered, "I don't know what to say... Forget it, nothing. Everything is fine."

He kissed me again to prove it but I pulled away this time. "No," I insisted, "tell me what's wrong."

"...I don't want you to get upset."

"Are you serious?"

"Or mad."

"Now I'm thinking the worst."

"I don't know what to say!" he sighed, exhaling a huge minty breath, "okay, sometimes... your breath smells."

"What!" I froze, my voice cracking, my breath hitching. No. Me? No.

"See, this is why I didn't want to say." He turned away again.

"No, stop! Like what? How bad?"

"I don't know! No, not horrible, just not specifically good. Actually, forget it. Forget I said anything."

"No," I said again, "Explain it. What's it like," I breathed into my hand and tried to smell, "it smells *now*?"

"Yes! Stop looking like that! It's not *horrible*. A bit sour? Like if we were talking normally it would be fine. But up close... you know, it kind of ruins the mood..."

"But I brush my teeth!"

"That's the problem." He groaned, "I don't think it's your mouth, maybe it's something you eat."

"Like what? I don't even eat garlic." I cried, my mind racing through all the foods I ate. Lots of fruits and vegetables. Sometimes pasta. Sometimes chicken. Cornflakes with milk.

"I don't know," Asher said, "you eat a lot of chocolate?"

"I love chocolate. You think it could be chocolate?"

"Maybe? You should check it up online."

"What can I do about it?" I brushed my teeth. I flossed. I didn't eat weird food. I've never felt so helpless in my life.

"I don't know, can you try mouthwash or something?"

"But I brush my teeth! Why isn't it enough?" I cried. Real tears, down my cheeks.

"Oh no, don't make me feel worse. Tell me something about me that bothers you. Anything. Do I smell weird? Do I chew loudly? Does my chest hair bother you?"

"No, you smell great," I sniffled, "and I love your chest hair." It was light and nice.

"It's okay, we'll go to the pharmacy and buy all the breath fresheners they have. Don't worry."

I cried harder. How long were we married? Six months? And Asher kept this hidden in him the whole time—me, his wife—and my helpless odor.

I was a horror story.

I sobbed.

Her Business

"By the way, my mother mentioned that you didn't call on Erev Shabbos…" it was Sunday evening. Miriam and I were unloading the groceries from the car when I remembered.

"Oh yeah!" Miriam said as she gently lifted a sleeping Chaim from his car seat, "I got caught up on the phone with my cousin Sima, the one who just got engaged. She wouldn't let me go until I practically hung up on her to light candles. She wanted all the juicy details on marriage—what's it like and is it worth it. She's terrified, poor girl."

I laughed as I closed the trunk, arms laden with shopping bags, "What did you tell her? To go ahead with it?"

"I did," Miriam smiled at me, "I told her it's the best decision I ever made."

I unlocked the door to our apartment as the plastic bags cut into my wrists. This apartment was ours for over two years but still felt so fresh and new.

It was two weeks to Pesach and half our counters were already covered. I emptied the bags onto the cleaned section as Miriam let Chaim down into his crib. Together we put the food away.

"You just know how my mom gets," I continue, rolling my eyes, "these little things, like Friday phone calls, mean a lot to her."

"Of course, I'm going to put her first on my list."

A week to Pesach and our kitchen was still only partially cleaned. Miriam's business had a lot of last-minute orders—she baked and sold boutique cookies—so we cleaned the best we could and set up the table and oven for her baking. We resigned to the last-minute stress of catching all the crumbs, scrubbing all the surfaces, and setting the oven for a long self-clean.

"It's a big *mitzvah* to start your cleaning early," my mother said over the line. She was watching Chaim this week so that Miriam could work.

"I know, I know. But what could I do?" I sighed, "We're starting to clean today. Nobody wants cookies any closer to Pesach anyways. Miriam finished her last batch and did the counters. How is Chaim?"

"What a darling boy! He ate some of my special eggy."

I shifted uncomfortably, Miriam told me specifically to make sure my mom knows not to feed Chaim eggs or honey or tuna or Bamba. He was nine months old and Miriam was hyper-careful with what he ate. I brought it up with my mom once but she just waved dismissively. "She's a new mother. It makes sense that she's worried. She reads all the stuff on the internet and in the books. But I raised seven of you with not one book and look at how you all turned out! Don't think I don't know what's good for your baby."

I didn't dare mention it to my mother again.

"I'll pick him up when I deliver the orders. I have to go. Miriam is calling me, she needs help with the mopping. We got this new type, a Swiffy I think it's called—"

"A Swiffer! I have one of those. Give her the phone, I'll explain it to her."

I went into the kitchen and put the phone by Miriam's ear, mouthing *mom.*

"Hi Mrs. Reich—Mom," Miriam hastily corrected herself. My mother always insisted that Miriam should call her *mom.* I don't know why but Miriam couldn't get the hang of it. My mother was really close to us, always helping out with Chaim and calling to see how we were doing. But that's the hardest part of marriage, I knew, taking two people from very different backgrounds and mixing them together. Sometimes it worked and a couple's lives meshed flawlessly. And sometimes it was like water and oil.

I kept mixing, hoping for the former.

"Yes, of course, I'm using a clean rag."

A pause. My mother spoke on the other end.

Miriam replied defensively, "I know I need to do a deeper clean for Pesach. I just want to go over the floors for now so it's decent. I'll do them again."

Another pause, longer this time.

"Thank you Mrs. Reich." Miriam said with a plastered on smile, "have a happy and kosher Pesach."

The second she hung up, she turned on me—

"What?" I backed away.

"She said 'I know how your floors can get a bit sticky.' Your mother hasn't been here in two weeks and the floors were spotless when she came! Why did she say our floors are sticky?"

I shrugged and desperately switched the topic, "any cookies for me to taste? You know—in the name of the business, just to make sure they came out good."

"No. There are only three extra and they are for me."

The next two days, Miriam was in wild haste to catch up on cleaning. Every time I saw her, she had a rag at hand and a different bottle of cleaning spray.

Finally she announced that she was done. The day of *bedikas chametz*. She put Chaim in a carriage and said she was going out.

"I can't stand to be in the kitchen a minute longer! I left chicken on the counter. It's for dinner. If you can throw something together…"

"Of course, you need a break. I'll take care of it."

The second she left I realized the misunderstanding. See, I'd assumed she meant *chicken*, chicken. Like prepared chicken. Like I'd just have to put some potatoes in the oven for a quick side dish. Nope, Miriam left me a slab of thawed chicken legs.

My thoughts raced.

"Mom, what's your recipe for chicken legs? The simple one... with the oven."

"Why in the name of *shamayim* do you need a recipe?"

"Miriam needed a break, she asked me to prepare for tonight." I poked the semi-defrosted chicken with a fork, "it can't be that hard, right?"

Four hours later, the table was set and Miriam was back. I proudly served her a plate of chicken with a side of sweet potatoes.

"Do you like it?" I pounced as soon as she took the first bite.

Miriam didn't speak. She stabbed a slice of sweet potato and bit into it.

"Is it fine? Is it cooked well?" I asked again. I had already actually tasted it before and I thought it tasted fine. More than fine actually. I was quite proud.

"Your mother called me," Miriam finally said quietly.

"Oh," I smiled, "that's nice."

"She asked why I don't cook for her son," Miriam burst, "I don't understand—why did you have to get her involved?!"

"Well... I just asked for a recipe."

"She thinks I'm a horrendous wife!"

"No, she doesn't! I tell her every day what amazing food you prepare!"

Miriam glared at her chicken.

Hey, I wanted to say, *I worked hard on this*. It was actually better than half the recipes Miriam used. This tasted homier. Perhaps it wasn't the best time to mention that she should try it out herself.

"Sorry," Miriam sighed, "I'm making a big deal out of this. I know you didn't mean to complain about me. These things just stress me out. Let's just try to keep some things to ourselves."

Our relationship was tense. I felt it. It was coming out in different ways—little arguments that would spur up—the chicken thing, the last-minute cleaning, heated discussions on who would take Chaim out. My mother said it might be because I'm home more—it was *bein hazmanim* and Miriam and I were seeing each other more than ever.

But I knew things were tense for another reason. One that was not at all Miriam's fault but I couldn't help blame her just a little.

It was an intimacy problem. Three weeks already, we hadn't touched. A few nights before *mikveh* night, Miriam called with the dreadful news, "I'm... I'm still unclean."

"Are you sure?" I pressed.

"You can ask the rabbi," she said helplessly, "but I'm almost positive."

She was right. Still unclean. And so we waited longer, the gap between our mattresses creating a tangible rift between us.

"Did she go to see her doctor about it?" my mother said on our daily phone call, "you know," she reminded, "this isn't the first time it's happened."

"I just don't know how to bring it up with her," I groaned. I was at loss for women's things.

My mother sighed, "do you want me to do it *zeeskeit*?

"That would be wonderful," I sighed, relief spreading to my toes. My mom was a supermom, she could take care of anything.

"Miriam! We're going to be late. Are you ready?" I called while tying my tie. It was *Erev* Pesach and we needed to get going if we wanted to get to my parents at a decent time.

"Miriam?"

She wasn't in the kitchen or the living room. The bathroom door was opened and empty. Only our bedroom door was shut.

"Miriam," I called and carefully opened the door.

The lights were shut and the shades drawn. It took a moment for my eyes to adjust and make out Miriam's form, lying flat on her bed, still in her *shmatte* clothes.

"What's going on? We have to leave soon."

"I can't speak to you," her voice was muffled in her pillow, "I can't even look at you—I'm so embarrassed!"

"What happened darling?" I turned on the light and sat at the edge of the bed. As close as was allowed.

She picked her face off the pillow and said, "I am not going to your parents. I can't bear to look at your mother."

"How could you say that?"

"How could she ask me about my *irregular bleeding?* Why does she know about that! I don't understand you. I know you two are close, but we're a couple! Just us two. Why is she always involved?

"She cares about you, she cares about us…"

"Well tell her to stop caring then! I've dealt with this for years but now you've crossed the line. I cannot stand the way you speak to your mother."

"Are you serious?" I didn't know what to think. This was a grown woman, this was my *wife*, and she was acting so immature, "my mom and I talk. Who cares? You and your mom talk too. And you know what? It's a good thing to speak to your parents! *Kibbud av v'eim*." Respect your father and mother, the most basic Torah commandment.

"I talk to my mom like a *normal* person. I don't tell her every detail of my life, and G-d knows I don't tell her about us!"

I flinched. It was the first time I heard Miriam speaking this way—using G-d's name in vain.

"So you're saying I'm not *normal* for having a good relationship with my mom?" I laughed incredulously, "Miriam, I really can't respect you with the way you are acting right now. You know I'm close to my mom, it's something I'm very proud of, and I hope you can develop that kind of thing with your own mother instead of putting me down."

"This is ridiculous," Miriam said, "leave the room. Get out!" she yelled when I didn't budge, "Run to mama. I'm taking Chaim to my parents."

"No," I said.

"Excuse me?"

"You are complaining that our life isn't 'private' enough and all of a sudden you are willing to make a whole huge scene? We are going to my parents tonight like we planned," my voice dropped in degrees, "If you don't accept my family, you don't accept me."

"What's that supposed to mean?"

"It's all or nothing, Miriam." I got up and went to the door, "You can't pick and choose. Me with my *mother* or nothing at all."

A half-hour later, Miriam emerged with red eyes, her long *sheitel* and a new dress.

"I am so upset at you," she whispered, as we took Chaim out to the car.

It was *niddah*. It made both of us tense. It made us argue so much more. It was the hardest part of being married, my mother assured me in the kitchen as I helped ladle the soup into bowls for *Shulchan Aruch*.

"Are you sure?" I said, biting my lip, "she barely spoke all through the *seder*."

"She just needs some time," my mother assured me, "I'll talk to her."

The Grass is Always Greener

"I'm listening, I'm listening," Aaron said, but a moment too late.

I rolled my eyes, "no you're not. You're not focused."

"You're overanalyzing me," Aaron leaned back and took another hit, "can you just chill?"

"I am chill! You're the one that's making me not chill," I folded my arms and shivered as the night air dropped a degree.

Aaron laughed, puffing smoke into the air, "I'm obviously smoking to relax. Maybe because it's not so easy to relax around here."

"So you're blaming me?" I asked incredulously.

That's it. I stood up and went inside, sliding the balcony door shut behind me. I didn't know why I even tried to spend time with him when he was like this. It always left me hurt and confused.

A moment before the door shut completely, he called, his voice ringing with laughter, "I'm not blaming you, *gosh*, don't take everything so personally."

But he still stayed outside, with his joint. His precious pot. And I stayed on the other side of the glass, watching for a moment, half hoping he would follow.

He didn't.

So I *did* take it personally.

It wasn't the first time Aaron had smoked at home. I didn't want to admit—recently it's been happening more often than not.

I remembered the first time I saw him smoke, just weeks after our wedding. It was the perfect autumn evening. We sat on our porch bathed in the full moon's light. The silver face grinned at us and I felt both minuscule and endless—as if it proved my insignificance in the world that was mine to take. I looked at Aaron and knew he felt it too. That this world that was *ours* to take, I corrected myself. We were a team, brand new and ready to take on *anything*.

Then Aaron brought it out.

I noticed when I saw the lighter's flame in his cupped hand.

"Are you *smoking*?" I'd asked, taken aback. Aaron and I had dated for three months, we got married after five. I was sure I knew everything there was to know about him but he never mentioned *smoking*.

"Don't worry, it's just weed," he'd smiled.

But that didn't calm me down. I watched as he expertly inhaled and exhaled a puff of smoke. Weed? As in *drugs*? Cigarettes I understood—addictive nicotine, ruins your lungs, but at least it doesn't alter your state of mind. But *drugs*? It was the thing off the blacklist, which our parents barely even warned us about because we were so far removed. *Drugs*? Street kids used it, the homeless begged for it, the hopeless died on it. *Drugs*? Not Aaron. Not my Aaron.

I thought back to every date, every conversation Aaron and I ever had. Were there any signs? Could I have predicted this? Would it helped if I had?

And now, what could I say? What should I do?

I didn't say a word, but my mind wouldn't shut up.

Aaron still watched the moon as he smoked, melting into his chair and sinking into the stars. I looked up too, but the universe didn't feel so comfortably endless anymore like it was ours to take. Now it just felt suffocatingly lonely.

I brought it up a few times after, each time with careful trepidation. Over dinner or Shabbat afternoon. When we were having a lovely time, *sober*.

He'd tell me funny stories, like about his Israeli uncle that taught in an American high school. He'd always say '*shit* of paper' instead of 'sheet of paper' and wouldn't get why the whole class cracked up. And I'd tell him sweet stories about the time my mom tracked down her childhood hero who survived the holocaust and moved to Israel. My mom got to speak to him just two months before he died. And Aaron and I both would lean forward, wanting to share more. To share everything.

And then, when we were comfortable and close and I looked into his eyes and knew I could say anything—then I'd speak.

"You don't think it... affects you negatively in any way?" I didn't want to come off as the stern wife. But I also wanted him to know that it bothered me. The way we'd have a perfect evening, talking, laughing, relaxing and just enjoying each other's presence. And then he'd get it out. His joint. A few puffs later and he'd retreat into his own world.

"You never smoked?" he'd say, "you just won't get it. You don't get how it feels."

"Yeah, but it's bad for you."

And that was when he'd start with me. My engineer husband all of a sudden turned into a top-class doctor, "actually, it's *not* bad for you. It doesn't do any harm to your lungs. It's way healthier than drinking and *that's* legal. And it's clinically proven to ease chronic pains. They even give it to veterans, it helps with all kinds of trauma. And depression, and insomnia too. It could even help you lose weight!"

"What about *you*?"

"What do you mean, what about me?"

"You don't have any chronic pains, you're not depressed or a veteran or an insomniac or whatever. Why do you smoke?"

He shrugged and said simply, "It makes me feel good."

My arguments died on my lips.

216

It took months for me to fully realize—it didn't make *me* feel good. Not at all.

When he'd come home after a particularly long day of work and I'd say, "How was work?"

And he'd irritably say, "You always ask me the same question," and, "why is there no orange juice?" and, "oh god, what a day."

In his sulky mood, folding his arms and turning away.

I'd prompt him again. Another conversation starter. What do you think of the name Sharon for a girl? Do you think we'll have lots of photo albums when we're older? When will we visit your mother? Anything.

"All you want to do is talk, talk, talk," Aaron mocked, "God, how much is there to talk about?"

It's true. That was all I wanted and he used to want it too! *Tell me about your day*, I wanted to beg, *if it's hard I can help you. We can talk this through.*

But on those nights it wasn't me that could comfort him. He'd be irritable until he lit up his joint and retreat onto the balcony into his own world. Yet, somehow still in front of me, still in our home. I'd busy myself around him, sweeping the balcony and the floor by his feet, so maybe he'd catch sight of the tears beading up in my eyes.

"Are you addicted?" I forced myself to ask. And it was true it didn't happen often, but once every few weeks was often enough for me

Aaron laughed, "It's just weed."

"So?" I didn't understand.

"I don't know why you treat me like I'm not some crazy drug addict. This is *weed*. It's legal in some states, and in a year or two it'll be legal all over America! It's safe and healthy and normal. That's right, it's *normal*." He stressed the word, "*Everyone* smokes. All my friends from high school smoke. We smoked a ton in yeshiva. We smoke. It's what people do."

He closed his red-rimmed eyes for a moment and I thought he was done, but then he added, "I'm sorry you're missing out on this global experience."

I pursed my lips and went back inside, refusing to let him make me feel clueless and dumb for an experience I did not want to have.

More and more, it was like another person in our relationship. Another body in our bed. Aaron had a new hobby and somehow that smoke that only took place every few months turned monthly, and then sometimes even twice a month.

Is this normal? I wanted to scream out into the world. Who could I ask? My mother? She would freak out more than me, she would call Aaron a hoodlum from the street and make me send him to rehab. I couldn't either bring it up with my best friend Tziporah. Her marriage was perfect. Like a mocking mirror of my own. We got married a month apart. Her husband was also an engineer. She was also a physical therapist like me. Her husband was a doll, nerdy with glasses and sweet. Probably never even heard of drugs in his life, let alone tried one.

Where did that leave me? In my own little world. This small, one-bedroom apartment with me, my husband and his pouch of weed.

The smell that made my stomach churn, the silence that made my ears ring—but it wasn't all bad! We did have good times, watching movies and eating sandwiches. Aaron was fine. It made him laugh, it made him comfortable. It made him feel good. Who was I to I stop him?

Who was I to let him?

No matter how much I tried intercepting my bad thoughts, nothing could hide how I really felt. It wasn't good.

I knew it. I knew it. I knew it. I didn't want him smoking anymore.

One night—one of *those* nights, exactly three weeks since the last smoke (yes, I tracked these things)—I finally put my foot down, "I don't want you smoking here anymore."

"Okay, okay," he put his hands up, "I'll close the door so it won't get inside."

"No," I stopped him, "I don't want you smoking in this house anymore. Porch or anywhere. If you want to smoke, don't do it around me. I can't be with you like this."

And Aaron stubbed his joint. He sat with me in the kitchen over the spaghetti I'd prepared and we spoke. We laughed. We dined like we always did on our good nights. I was all grins and laughs. And funny stories and sweet stories, and his day at work went well, they're making so much progress. My day went well too, I'm happy you care.

I was proud of myself. All I had to do to break the barriers of miscommunication was use my words and ask—

"I have to step out," he stood up in middle, "actually, I decided it really bothers me that you're trying to control me."

I didn't stop him. I did cry.

The rest of the week, Aaron came home later and later.

"Where did you go?" I asked, in bed but awake and waiting. Running my fingers through my hair, biting my nails, scrolling endlessly on my phone. Waiting.

"Friends," he shrugged, "you don't let me be me at home so I'll be me somewhere else."

"High you is the only you?" I asked.

"Are you serious? I'm just hanging out. You know I literally get high *once* a month. Not even—"

"Last month you got high twice," I whispered.

"And the way you're acting and *stressing* me makes me want to get high a *whole* lot more," Aaron snapped, "I'm not your kid and you can't control me, just like I don't try controlling *you* when something *you* does bothers *me*. And believe me, you are *far* from perfect yourself."

Aaron didn't wait for me to answer. He got up and moments later I heard the balcony door slide open. The rest is history.

What did I do? Stinging, stinging, stinging. Of course, I cried.

Give Me a Break

I heard the lock twist and the door open. My darling husband had arrived! I glanced in the mirror above the bathroom sink to adjust my snood and went out to greet him.

"Ahh," Simcha inhaled deeply as he strode in, "my favorite smell."

The house did smell overwhelmingly *yummy*. Six challahs in the oven. The air was thick with the scent, as it was every Thursday evening.

"Did you work hard today?" I pulled out a chair for Simcha and went back to my opened cookbook on the counter.

"No," Simcha looked around the kitchen, appraisingly, "but I'm sure you did."

I rolled my eyes. Simcha always made light of the social work he did. He was such a hard worker and a true gentleman. I peeked at him as I got the flour and sugar out. He looked so handsome with his cropped beard. It made him seem older than his twenty-three years. Older and wiser.

It was true though, I did work hard. I scrubbed our house from top to bottom, helped a neighbor out with the kids because their twelve-year-old twisted his ankle and they had to rush with him to the emergency room. And the shopping for Shabbos, and the cooking of course.

"You know that apartment three doors down?" I said as I flipped through the cookbook to the most worn and stained page. My favorite *babka* recipe.

"Oh yeah, a new family moved in last week. The Applebaums."

"You knew and didn't tell me?" I narrowed my eyes, "I just met Shira Applebaum in the supermarket and couldn't believe she lived right here—I feel so horrible I didn't make them a welcome *babka* yet."

"Well, I'm sure they'll be happy to get one in time for Shabbos."

"Are you hungry?" I remembered to ask, "Why don't you grab something from the fridge?"

Simcha opened the fridge and peeked in the pans. Most of it was raw—food for Shabbos that I'd prepared to put in the oven tomorrow. I bit my lip and tried to think of what I can feed him.

"Oh no, not that." I called over Simcha's shoulder as he glass container he took out full of meatballs, "That's for Penina Rosen. She just had a new baby *baruch Hashem*, a boy. The *bris* is on Wednesday. I organized a food train and I'm first—she's already coming home tonight! Wants to be home for Shabbos."

"Maybe I'll just take one, and a bit of the spaghetti?"

"No, no. It's for her whole family, she has two other kids you know."

"There's nothing else... I'll have cereal?"

"Don't be silly," I went to the fridge and looked inside, "here, some cheese, sauce. Let's make you a pizza bread. I'll have some too. I'm actually *craving* it."

I tested the word out, 'craving.' I was four months pregnant *baruch Hashem* and I felt energized and full of life. Was I craving pizza bread? It did sound good. Simcha wasn't as excited about the pizza bread. I put a hand on his arm and consoled him, "We'll have real food tomorrow night, so don't worry. You can't eat *fleish* every night—you'd never have an appetite for my chicken soup that way!"

"Don't you know?" he smiled and got plates for our pizzas, "I always have an appetite for your chicken soup."

I wrapped the challahs carefully, "now take these to the Fishmans, this to the Kleins, the Rosens of course, and now the Applebaums too. Oh, and you said you want to bring two to your parents. It's a really good idea, they will be so happy."

"You're such a *tzadekes*," Simcha said fondly as I packed the challah in bags, "did you eat, are you okay?" and of course he had to add, "I think you're working too hard."

"Oh, stop it you."

"Wait," Simcha said as I packed the last one, "that's all the challah. What about for us?"

"It's alright," I waved my hand dismissively, "You can stop by the bakery on the way home and buy some rolls. We don't need much."

But Simcha wouldn't budge, "It's not the same as your challah."

"*We* have my challah every week," I gave him a little shove, "now go make others happy."

"We didn't have your challah for weeks. I want you to have it. It's healthier, better for the baby…"

"The baby can handle it," I snapped impatiently, "what should I do, take one from your parents? You told them you'd send it and I can only make so many challahs."

Simcha sighed and took the bags,

I watched him go, my frown deepening. I didn't know what had gotten into him lately but he had this bitterness to him.

Simcha left in the morning and came straight back, not ten minutes later.

"Did you forget something?" I asked. He'd caught me just before I started *davening*.

"Where is the car?" he demanded, "I can't find the car. I went up and down this block like a *meshuga* looking for it."

"I lent it to Ester Kesselman for the week," Simcha didn't react so I gabbed on, "You know her aunt is visiting from New York. They wanted to take her around. We're so fortunate your parents bought us the car, aren't we? Hashem does such *chesed* for us, I wanted to share it with other people."

"That's great," he said through tight teeth, "Except I need it to get to work."

"Where's Yaakov? You always get a ride with him."

"*He* is out of the country for the week."

"Well, how could I have known?" I shrugged. Our neighbor, Yaakov Frish worked in the same office. Simcha *always* got a ride and left the car with me for errands. I didn't mind forgoing the luxury for one week.

"You could have *asked* me?" he said it as a question. I suppose I could have asked… but what bothered me more was how he was making such a big deal out of this—like this was my plot to sabotage him! It was an honest mistake and Simcha could act less self-centered. I clutched my *siddur* tightly in my hands and said, "It's a twenty-five-minute walk. You can't walk for a few days?"

"A few days?" Simcha sputtered. He didn't wait for an answer, just slammed the door shut behind him.

The anger wasn't good for me. I opened my *siddur* and tried to focus on the words, on the meaning, on the G-d above that ran the intricacies of this world.

The week passed in a blur. In between helping Mrs. Silverstein, the elder woman who lived ten minutes away, with the cleaning and some cooking, and sewing for the *gemach*, I barely had time for anything else. I helped out at a clothing *gemach* three afternoons a week. Mrs. Eidelstein, the woman who ran in—now *she* was a real *tzadekes*—couldn't deal with everything on her own. The sorting, the hanging, the sewing, the selling. It was the least I could do to take some of the work home with me.

Simcha, of course, had what to say on that too.

"I have this shirt that's missing a button." He said when he saw me surrounded by clothes with my sewing kit out, "Would you mind fixing it on?"

"You don't see I have a million things to sew?" I gestured to all the clothes. It would take hours. Of course, Simcha was dumping his own things on me too, when usually he sewed his buttons just fine himself. I softened a little at his sad face, "I'll try next week though. Leave it on the shelf."

"You work too hard," he said. But this time it didn't sound like a compliment. He said it cold and harsh, and left me alone in the room. I bit my lip and focused hard on stitching second-hand overalls.

And now it was Thursday again. I had my phone lodged between my ear and shoulder as I put the trays of challah

228

into the oven, speaking to Simcha on the line, "Can you stop by and bring chicken on the way home? The Applebaums are coming for the meal Friday night."

"You didn't tell me they were coming."

"You suggested we invite them!" I knew what was starting before it even started and I was exasperated already.

"Well, you should have told me you actually did," said this new Simcha.

"What does it matter?"

"I don't know. You made a big deal that I didn't tell you when they moved in. I'm allowed to make a big deal that they're eating in our house."

I took the phone away from my ear for a moment, startled, "I don't know if you're serious or not, but if you are I am really shocked."

"Shocked at what? That your husband wants to be considered, at least some of the time."

"I really can't have this conversation now..." I looked at the challah in the oven. A teacher from high school once told me I should think only positive things when the challah is baking. "We'll talk later tonight."

"By the way," Simcha added, "it would be easier to stop by the supermarket with *A CAR*. Now I'll have to lug raw chicken home."

He hung up.

Later tonight came all too soon. I dressed the chicken and put it to roast, chopped vegetables in narrow tins, prepared all the salads I could...

And all the while, Simcha waited patiently on the kitchen chair. The moment I sat down, he started, "It's too much. You're too much. You're helping everyone so much, you don't even have time to help me... or us."

"Oh," I said slowly and looked around, "so this house just cleaned itself, did it? The food for Shabbos just magically appeared in the fridge as well?"

"Okay, okay," he shook his head, "but what about when I'm hungry, or tired, or just need something from you— you'd always rather help someone else."

"That is not true!" I jumped to my feet, "I see how you twist things to fit your story. Don't think I don't notice. You want our home to be open and giving but the second you have to compromise even a *tiny* bit—you pull back. Well, that's what giving is about—compromises."

"I am willing to compromise!" on his feet as well, "But let me choose! Don't force them on me."

"You're right, I can't force anything," I blinked and looked away from him, "it's just heartbreaking when you thought you shared values with someone."

"It's heartbreaking when your own wife would rather help the whole world in its entirety, than help her own husband."

"Stop making this about you."

"This is *only* about me! I'm telling you how I feel."

"And I'm telling you that you're reading things the wrong way. This stress isn't good for me," I put a hand on my stomach and sat down.

"Are you okay?" and suddenly he was at my side.

"I'm fine, I'm fine," I waved him away.

"Can I just say one last thing?" he said after a minute.

"It's a free country Simcha. Say what you want."

"You know on an airplane, you put your mask on before helping others?"

I nodded.

"That's it. You have to help yourself first."

I looked him square in the eye and said, "My mask is always on. I breathe a Torah life and I breathe through *mitzvos*. I thought you were the same. I thought we were on the same page. It used to feel like we were. Now? I don't know anymore."

I refused to let Simcha ruin everything—the challah, the help I gave Mrs. Silverstain, or my sewing for the *gemach*, or baking for the community. I refused to let Simcha taint these good deeds with his selfishness. And yet... I had to make peace with him somehow.

"I saved you a challah," I told him as we crawled into bed. Really, it was for the Friday night meal with the Applebaums, but this way I could please two parties with one challah.

Simcha turned over to look at me and smiled, "that means a lot to me. Thank you."

Late to the Game

You see all these young wives with stars in their eyes, shopping the world for their new homes. Always radiating a secret sort of joy. You could spot them on line at the fish store, complaining loudly yet proudly about the guests they'd host on Shabbos, or at the nail salon walking to the back room for an extensive waxing. You bumped into them at the bakery, "*my husband loves his chocolate danish*," or heard their voices in the changing rooms at malls, "do you think Yitzy will like *this*?" They were always flitting, always busy, always happy and always somewhat mysterious.

I've watched these women for years—at least ten. At first these women were my friends, getting married and experimenting with smooth *sheitels* and more makeup than ever before. Eventually, they moved past the stage of newlywed, gaining a comfortable amount of weight and settling into elastic skirts. Then, a new generation of young brides took their place and I'd watch them just as keenly.

At age twenty-two. I was happy for them. When I turned twenty-six, I was curious about them, anticipating. By twenty-seven, jealous, when would it be my turn? At twenty-nine, I gave up hope, or was it by twenty-eight?

And at thirty it happened! At last!

Everyone said it would—when you least expect it. When you give up hope.

Finally, I joined the league of starry-eyed girls—except, I realized with a tightening in my chest, it wasn't all that exciting like they made it out to be.

Menachem, my husband, was a good man. Thirty-two at the time. He had a beard but kept it trimmed, never married. Little ambition and a big heart.

We were married for nearly two years now, had one beautiful little boy and another baby on the way—I had to make up for lost time, didn't I? We were happy together, but ecstatic? Starry-eyed? Cloud nine? Maybe during the wedding. After that it was just... okay.

Mikveh was annoying, sex was nice but nowhere near the hype. Sharing a bed was overwhelming, even after blocking out his snores with earplugs, he'd tug at my blanket and wake me up. Eventually, we'd just left the beds separate. Sharing a car was stressful, especially sharing my perfect new Volkswagen Beetle. But it didn't make sense to buy a second car for our small family.

Sharing a house was stressful too:

"Did you never hear of taking your shoes off before you step inside? Your shoes are filthy!"

"I'm stepping on the floor. Floors are supposed to be dirty."

"No, they are not." I pointed at the shoe rack beside the door, put there for this exact purpose.

Two years, it was still a struggle. He always had a hasty excuse: "I'm just running in for a second," or, "I'm going out soon. It'll take me five minutes just to undo the laces."

Or the way he cooked with spicy pepper.

"I can't eat it this way," I'd spit out his soup and douse my tongue with water.

"I can't eat it any other way."

Or the way he seemed so helpless with everything but his guitar.

Marriage wasn't easy and husbands definitely weren't easy either. I don't want to be the Debby-downer, crashing the married people's party too late and complaining the whole way—and it's not like I didn't know there would be struggles, I just wish someone honestly told me beforehand how hard it was going to be. Next time I meet a *kallah*, I'll sure let her know.

The week of *sheva brachos* was akin to plunging into ice cold water. I remember the shock of it until this day.

We'd moved into our apartment together the day after the wedding. I had set it up meticulously the two weeks before to make sure each tiny detail was exactly how I liked. But suddenly, with this second presence in the room... it all felt different. Out of place. He sat on the couch, ruffled the carefully arranged pillows and said, "Wow, this place looks great. We actually *own* it?"

"*I* own it," I said without thinking and immediately regretted it, "I mean I bought it for us. Now it's ours," I smiled weakly.

It was a good deal and my second property. The first was just for investment, a house in Pennsylvania. I hadn't meant to purchase another so soon, especially weeks before the wedding and without consulting my *chosson*, but it also seemed irrelevant at the time. Why should I consult with Menachem what to do with the money *I'd* saved for the past ten years?

It was a hard topic to discuss at first—finances—but we found a way to comfortably express how we felt: "No way did I agree to marry your debt." I came into this marriage with a nice savings and two properties. Menachem dropped out of college and didn't pay back his loans.

"Okay then," he said, "I'll pay off my own debt but you take care of the mortgage and the bills..."

So it was agreed, our bank accounts remained separate. Sometimes Menachem borrowed from me to cover his expenses of the month, but I made him track it on Splitwise. It was time he learned a bit about finances.

And then it was evening. Our second evening together and the first evening together in our home. Menachem pulled out his phone and put on a video. The lights flashed through the pitch-black room.

My eyes widened. Our beds were too far apart for me to see what he was watching.

I heard a purr from the phone.

"What is that?" I said in a squeak.

"Animal planet."

"Now? It's past midnight. Let's go to sleep." I said to the dark.

After a moment, he said, "I can't fall asleep without it."

"What do you mean?"

"I always watch Animal Planet before I go to bed. I used to really suffer from insomnia, but with this I just fall straight to sleep."

"What about Shabbos?" I challenged.

"It's the one night I could do without. I don't know how, my body is just used to it I guess."

The narrator said, "Look at that, a real live bobcat!"

"You can't wear headphones?" I said, desperately.

"Well," he said slowly, "I don't want to fall asleep with them and choke. Does it bother you that much?

"Yes, Menachem, it really does."

When he finally dozed off, the snoring started. The whole night I listened to the orchestra of disrupted breathing pipes.

By now I already had earplugs to stuff my ears and a fluffy eye mask. Menachem and I had chosen it together on Amazon. He wanted to get the creepy ones with an open eye illustration on it. I opted for pink and soft. I was the one paying for it after all.

Another issue that came up was the whole last name thing. The plaque on my—our?—door said Stein.

"Are we going to change that to Reichenstein?" Menachem asked me. Of course his last name was not of the short and sweet type.

I sighed, "Look, Stein is basically like Reichenstein...just much shorter and nicer. I think we should keep this for now."

It's been two years. The kids have Reichenstein on their birth certificates but my ID and my front door refuse to change from plain and easy Stein.

Two years later, I stepped into our bedroom after putting our baby to sleep, my stomach already swelled large. Menachem was on the bed distracted by his phone.

"You're wearing outside clothing on the bed again!"

This was another one of those small constant struggles between us. Like, *EW*, change your clothing when you come inside the house and especially when you lay on the place where you sleep. "Seriously," I said, "you're being plain old disgusting. Our sheets are going to smell!"

Yeah, people definitely hyped this marriage thing up. I went to go yell at him.

Anniversary Day

"This *Rosh Chodesh* will be our fortieth anniversary," Shaindle announced over breakfast one Sunday morning. She was going over her calendar, filling out dates and marking appointments as she did every morning.

"Is it?" Zev looked up from the newspaper, "where did the time go?"

Shaindle looked around their home. The home they've built for forty years. (Metaphorically speaking, as they've only lived in this particular house for fifteen.) Forty years, seven children and eleven grandchildren later. All the kids moved out. Levy, the youngest, had set off for yeshiva in Israel just two weeks ago.

"Should we go out to celebrate?" Shaindle wondered, "We can do something special."

"Maybe we can invite the kids over, have a big meal," Zev suggested. It was always nice to have the kids around. The kids brought *their* own kids and suddenly the house was alive again.

"Michal and Shifra are away for the summer, Danny won't want to travel for four hours with the kids. Neither will Huvie want to travel. Levy is in Israel. Who does that leave us with? Shimon and his wife? They're newlyweds, let's leave them alone for a bit."

"Of course. So it's just us."

"Just us," Shaindle repeated.

The table was silent again, Shaindle busy with her calendar and Zev with his newspaper.

The problem with Sundays was that they were impossibly long. At least on Shabbos, it was customary to invite guests and spend the whole afternoon entertaining another couple from *shul* and their kids, or a neighbor, or a childhood friend, or their own children bringing along their spouses and the precious grandchildren.

On Sundays, Shaindle and Zev had no one to entertain but each other.

"Did you call Huvie recently? I didn't hear from her." Zev said from his couch to hers. She liked to sit on the loveseat. He always sat on the recliner.

"I called her an hour ago. She's trying to adjust to her new apartment and roommates."

"I don't like that she's so far away."

"Me neither." Shaindle agreed.

"Twenty years old! A girl should live at home until she's married." Zev ranted on.

Forty years spent with not a moment to breathe. When they got married Zev was twenty-two, Shaindle was just eighteen. Barely nine months after the wedding, they had their first child. Their first few years together were spent in a craze of working long hours and parenting three babies, born one after another. And then, slowly, after a break of two years, and then three, they added new additions to the clan, still worked as hard, still fought to raise their kids in the way of Hashem. Babies were hard, toddlers were impossible. Kids were stressful. But teenagers were the worst.

Side by side Zev and Shaindle got through it all. Through eating pasta every night for dinner that time Zev got laid off and they had to make do with less, through the trip to Washington D.C with all the kids one *chol hamoed*, through fights with Shifra over the man she wanted to marry and arguments with Huvie on the way she dressed and talks with Danny on what kind of life he wanted to lead.

Side by side they created life—a home always bursting with energy.

And now the kids were gone and Zev and Shaindle were still side by side. There was just less to get through now. The mortgage was paid off. The kids were far away. They both worked from Monday through Friday and went to *shiurim* in the evenings—separately.

Nothing new.

"I'm going out to some stores," Shaindle said. It was late afternoon. Going out passed the time better than sitting home like a klutz.

"We're out of pickles."

"I know."

A foot out the door, Shaindle turned back, "why don't we go out together?"

"I don't like shopping."

"Oh," Shaindle said, thoughtfully, "What do you like?"

"Hmm, that's a good question. I never really thought about it."

He came up with an answer by the time she got back with the pickles and other few items from the grocery store.

"I really like hiking."

"You? Hiking? You never hiked a day in your life!"

"I used to," Zev nodded, "In summer camps."

"Which summer camps?"

"I must have told you about them. I'd go every summer." He never told her, so now he did.

And then Zev asked Shaindle, "What do you like? Besides shopping."

"You know what I like. Redecorating. Sewing. Cooking. Reading."

"That's it?"

"That's not enough?" Shaindle demanded. It took Zev an hour to come up with one thing! But then she remembered, "I also like painting."

"You paint?"

"I used to."

It was nice, to look at the person sitting across from you. The same face you've woken up to, day in, day out, for forty years, and to suddenly see something new. Something in the way his eye crinkled when he remembered. Something in the faint lines by her mouth when she thought.

"Maybe one Sunday we should hike together?" Shaindle suggested.

"No, I have a bad knee now," Zev said, "but maybe we can paint together?"

Shaindle shook her head, "Too messy. But," she added with a shy smile, "It's nice to just talk. To get to know you better."

She expected Zev to say something like, "forty years! You know me plenty!" But he didn't. He just smiled shyly back and nodded in agreement.

Glossary

The following glossary provides a partial explanation of some of the Hebrew, Yiddish, and Aramaic words and phrases used in this book. The spelling and explanations reflect the way the specific word is used herein. Often, there are alternate spellings and meanings for the words.

Abba: father

Asher Yatzar: blessing customarily said after using the bathroom

Ayin hara: the evil eye

Badatz: highest Kosher standard

Baruch Hashem (abbreviated B"H): Thank G-d

Bein Hazmanim: vacation time for Yeshivas

Bench: to recite the blessing after meals

Binah: understanding

Bochur: a young man

Bracha/brachos: blessing/s

Bris: the circumcision/circumcision ceremony

Bubby: grandmother

Chas v'shalom: G-d forbid

Chavrusa/chavruta: a Torah study partner

Chuppah: the wedding canopy

Chatan/chosson: groom

Chevre: close friends

Daven: pray

Dikduk: Hebrew grammer

Dvar Torah: words of Torah

Emunah: faith

Eretz Yisroel: Israel

Fleish: meat

Frum: religious

Gemach: fund offering free loans

Goyish: non-Jewish

Halacha: Jewish law

Hashem: G-d

Hashgacha pratis: Divine guidance

Hashkafa: outlook on levels of observance

Havdalah: blessing recited to conclude the Shabbat Heter: rabbinic allowance

Hechsher: Kosher certification

Hishtadlus: effort

Im yirtze Hashem (abbreviated I"H) : if G-d wills it

Ima: mother

Kallah: bride

Kavanah: sincere intention

Kibbud av v'eim: the Torah commandment to honor ones mother and father

Ketubah: marriage contract

Kevarim: gravesites

Kiddush: sanctification of the Sabbath and festivals usually recited over a cup of wine or grape juice

Kollel: institute for full-time, advanced study of the Talmud and rabbinic literature

Kumzitz: a musical gathering

Makolet: convenience store

Makpid: stringent

Mazal tov: phrase to express congratulations

Middah/middos: virtue/s

Mincha: afternoon prayer

Minhag/im: custom/s

Min haShamayim/miShamayim: from G-d

Mitzvah/mitzvos: commandment/s, popularly understood as a good deed

Motzei Shabbos: Saturday evening

Neshama: soul

Niddah: The time, usually lasting twelve days to fourteen days, when Jewish law forbids conjugal relations

Nisayon: test or trial

Oleh chadash: new immigrant to Israel

Oneg Shabbos: celebratory gathering held on Shabbos

Parsha: weekly Torah portion

Perek: chapter

Pru Urvu: the Torah commandment to have children

Shkiyah: sunset—marking the start of Shabbat

Shkoyach: (expression) may it be for strength

Shlumpy: slovenly

Shmatte: a rag or shabby garment

Shmiras Einaim: the act of protecting one's eyes from unholy images

Shtus: nonsense

Shulchan Aruch: the main and most widely consulted collection of Jewish law

Shvimkleid: a swim dress

Taharas Hamishpacha: the family laws of purity that prohibit conjugal relations during the niddah period

Talmidim: students

Teudat Zehut: Israeli identity document

Rav: a rabbi

Rebbe: teacher or mentor

Seder: time devoted to learning during the day

Sefer: holy book

Sem: abbreviated seminary

Sheva brachos: the week of celebration after the wedding

Sfira/Sfirat ha'Omer: The counting of the Omer. A period of time between Pesach and Shavuot

Shachris: morning prayer

Shadchan/shadchanit: matchmaker

Shamayim: the heavens

Shechita: method of Kosher slaughter

Shayach: relevant

Sheitel: wig

Shidduch/shidduchim: marriage proposals

Shidduch Crisis: The Shidduch crisis is a commonly observed and discussed phenomenon in the Orthodox Jewish community whereby eligible single persons, especially women, have difficulty finding a suitable spouse

Shiur: lesson

Shkoyach: the condensed version of the Hebrew phrase *yashar koach*, literally meaning "May you have strength" although commonly used as a way of saying "good job".

Shmone Esrei: the silent, standing prayer

Shomer (negiah): the halachic prohibition on touching members of the opposite sex

Shul: a synagogue

Tachlis: the real deal

Taharas mishpacha: laws of family purity in accordance with Jewish law

Tatty: daddy

Taiva: desire

Teshuva: repentance

Tichel: headscarf worn my married women

Treif: non-kosher

Tzitzis: specially knotted ritual tassels worn under clothing

Tznius: modesty

Yeshiva: an academy of Torah study

Yerushalayim: Jerusalem

Yetzer Hara: evil inclination

Yiddeshe neshama: Jewish soul

Yiras shamayim: fear of G-d

Yontif: holiday

Zeeskeit: (term of endearment) sweetie

Yay! You finished this book!

If you have a minute, it would mean so much to me if you would review this book online—on Amazon or Goodreads. Your review goes a long way toward encouraging other people to read #ShidduchCrisis and #ShalomBayis, and I'd consider it a *huge personal favor*.

Thank you in advance!

And please send any questions, comments, edits, or feedback to:

Peninashtauber@gmail.com

Sincerest thank!
Penina

About the Author

Penina Shtauber holds a BFA from Bezalel Academy of Art and Design. In her free time, she enjoys writing, reading, working on films, running, travelling and too many more hobbies to list. She grew up in New York and lives in Israel.

Ingram Content Group UK Ltd.
Milton Keynes UK
UKHW021051100423
419916UK00014B/527